D0893434

# OF MICE AND METAPHORS

Other Books by Jerrold R. Brandell

*Countertransference in Psychotherapy with
    Children and Adolescents* (contributing editor)
*Narration and Therapeutic Action* (editor)
*Theory and Practice in Clinical Social Work*
    (contributing editor)

# O F  M ICE
# AND
# METAPHORS

THERAPEUTIC STORYTELLING

WITH CHILDREN

JERROLD R. BRANDELL, PH.D.

A Member of the Perseus Books Group

Published by Basic Books,
A Member of the Perseus Books Group

A CIP catalog record for this book is available from the Library of Congress.
ISBN 0-465-00712-0

Design by Elizabeth Lahey

00 01 02 03 / 10 9 8 7 6 5 4 3 2 1

*Dedicated in Loving Memory to My Parents*
*Jules Brandell*
*and*
*Edna Bernice Honoroff*

# Contents

# Acknowledgments

**M**uch of the research for this book was completed during a semester-long sabbatical I spent in 1999 at the University of Canterbury as a Visiting Professor of Social Work. I wish first of all to thank my family for accompanying me abroad and thereby making this possible. My wife and partner, Esther, my daughter, Andrea, and my two sons, Joey and Stevie, have each had a significant share in this product, and I am extremely grateful to them for their love and endurance throughout our five months together in New Zealand.

I also wish to express my appreciation to Dr. Dugald McDonald, head of the Department of Social Work at the University of Canterbury, for the invitation to spend my sabbatical at Canterbury. I am likewise indebted to Dr. Leon W. Chestang, former Dean of the Wayne State University School of Social Work, for his encouragement and support of my sabbatical plans. Thanks are also due to my good friend and colleague Associate Professor Ken Daniels for his gracious generosity and incomparable Kiwi wit, and to Canterbury faculty members Marie Connolly and Kate van Heugten, as well as doctoral fellow Andrew Frost, for their collegiality and friendship throughout my stay in Aotearoa. I am particularly grateful to Kate van Heugten for her creative reading of the case of Mattie in Chapter 6. And I thank Ainsley Oberg for both her technical assistance and her kindness, despite the fact that my research requirements at times added considerably to her workload.

I also wish to acknowledge a debt to my teachers, close friends, and colleagues at the Michigan Psychoanalytic Council, where I have been privileged to study psychoanalysis in a rarefied intellectual climate during the past six years. I am especially indebted to Drs. Bert Karon, Henry Krystal, Murray Meisels, Jack Novick, and Norman Gordon for their contributions to my development as a psychoanalytic clinician.

I have also benefited from being able to present many of the ideas contained within this book to countless social work graduate students, who over the years have enrolled in my course on child and adolescent psychotherapy and with whom I have enjoyed a stimulating and at times provocative intellectual discourse.

I owe a considerable debt of gratitude to my editor at Basic Books, Cindy Hyden, for her early interest and enthusiasm in this project, as well as for the thoroughness, creativity, and consummate professionalism with which she approached the editorial task.

Finally, I would like to acknowledge the influence and early encouragement of Dr. Richard Gardner, whose seminal work on the *mutual storytelling technique* stimulated and shaped my own interest in children's narratives while I was engaged in doctoral research at the University of Chicago in the late 1970s.

The cases I use to illustrate techniques of metaphorical communication with children are drawn from twenty-three years of practice experience in several different clinical venues (family service, community mental health, outpatient child psychiatry, and private practice), reflecting the way my own clinical approach has evolved. I am especially grateful to the scores of young storytellers who over the years have invited me to participate in their very private fantasies and, in the process, have helped me to become a better listener and therapist.

Many of the chapters that follow are revised and, in some cases, expanded versions of papers I have previously published in the following journals: "Stories and Storytelling in Child Psychotherapy," *Psychotherapy*, *21*, 154–162 (Spring 1984 [copyright (1984) by Division of Psychotherapy of the American Psychological Association]); "Using Children's Autogenic Stories in Dynamic Clinical Assessment," *Child and Adolescent Clinical Social Work Journal*, *2*, 181–190 (Fall 1985); "Autogenic Stories and Projective Drawings: Tools for the Clinical Assessment and Treatment of Severely Disturbed and At-Risk Children," *Journal of Independent Social Work*, *1*, 19–32 (Winter 1987); "Narrative Truth and Historical Truth in Child Psychotherapy," *Psychoanalytic Psychology*, *5*, 241–257 (Summer 1988); "Treatment of the Bi-Racial Child: Theoretical and Clinical Issues," *Journal of Multicultural Counseling and Development*, *16*, 113–134 (Winter 1989); "Psychotherapy of a

Traumatized Ten Year Old Boy: Theoretical Issues and Clinical Considerations," *Smith College Studies in Social Work*, *62*, 123–138 (March 1992); and "Using Children's Autogenic Stories to Assess Therapeutic Progress," *Journal of Child and Adolescent Psychotherapy*, *3*, 285–292 (October 1986).

# Prologue

---

*Once upon a time there was a cat who lived in a lost
alley, and he was all alone. . . .*

So began one of the first stories presented to me
during a therapy hour. Ever since that clinical
encounter in the mid-1970s, I have been fasci-
nated by the creative ways in which children are able
to narrate their lives through imaginative storytelling.
These are stories that are intensely personal and often
filled with high drama; they are rich with dynamic
meaning, important themes and conflicts, and efforts
at resolution and adaptation. Like the dreams that are
Freud's "royal road to the unconscious," the make-
believe stories of children offer the listener an unsurpassed opportunity to enter a domain of childhood
usually off-limits to grown-ups.

Actually, children's stories represent an aspect of intrapsychic life and a mode of expression that for most
adults has become rather unfamiliar. I refer to the psychoanalytic notions of *primary* and *secondary process*.
Although some confusion exists as to how one applies
these concepts to particular mental phenomena, they
are very much alive and well and uniquely relevant to

our work with children. Primary process is, in effect, the lost language of childhood; it is the language of play and imagination, of creativity, and of action and impulse; it is what I shall term the language of mice and metaphors. It is a natural language that is often closely linked to the unconscious realm of mental life and dominated by the pleasure principle.

As we grow older, we gradually enter a different domain, one where logic, order, and the syntactic and semantic aspects of verbal expression are more highly prized. This is the language of adulthood, of secondary process; in a sense, it represents something of a compromise. In order to function in the adult world, we must give up or at least substantially alter a mode of expression that represents the un-self-conscious spontaneity of childhood. This is necessary because we must all somehow communicate with each other in a meaningful way, make sense of what we read in the morning newspaper, know how to insert a disk into our computers, and so on.

But we shouldn't require children, at least before a certain age, to do this. In fact, one noted child developmentalist (Elkind, 1989) has strongly cautioned parents not to make excessive academic, social, and other performance demands of developing children. In our assiduous efforts to prepare children for the challenges they will face as adults, however, we often fail to heed this advice; we tend, in fact, to increase our demands, regulating and directing not only their work but also their play. So intent are we in providing them with all the best opportunities that we may forget that our children also require privacy, a less-closely monitored

*Spielraum* within which they can develop their own personal narratives and potentials. We may no longer be able to speak their language, the language of primary process, with fluency; yet, on the other hand, we must be careful not to ask them to leave behind this domain prematurely.

It has been said that children are natural storytellers. They certainly enjoy listening to stories and (in my own clinical experience, at least) often find pleasure in being able to compose their own. Of course, no single technique used in clinical work with children is failsafe, or yields the same results for most children, or even yields the same results for the same child at different points in the course of therapy. Storytelling is no exception to this general rule, although when it works, it is unsurpassed as a means for assisting children to narrate their lives. Because we live in an age when public and private agencies and consumers have come to expect instant solutions to problems, it is far more difficult to promote the idea that we must listen carefully to children. As child psychotherapists we know that meaningful communication in therapy has a life and rhythm of its own, that a child's narrative evolves or unwinds in its own way and at its own pace. Imaginative stories thus permit us the opportunity not only to immerse ourselves in a child's fantasy world but also to engage in a therapeutic dialogue as eloquent as it is timeless.

# CHAPTER I

# Stories and Reciprocal Storytelling in Dynamic Child Psychotherapy

The significant differences in psychotherapy with children, adolescents, and adults have multiple ramifications for the ways in which we approach the treatment process. As a general rule, few adolescents and even fewer children express interest in discussing their wishes or intrapsychic conflicts, nor are most very receptive to this idea. Not unrelatedly, the overwhelming majority of children and adolescents do not usually seek out psychotherapy independently for themselves but, rather, are brought, sometimes quite unwillingly, into treatment by their parents. Moreover, children and adolescents reside in an environment that has become a historical milieu for the adult patient: Children and adolescents are in the process of negotiating in real time those conflicts and crises that for the adult patient are only variously accessible memories. Children and adolescents are in effect still heavily engaged with both parents and siblings in multiple discourses that for most adults may have come to exist only at the level of the imaginary.

Aside from these distinctions and many others that we might focus on, there is a fundamental difference in the repertoire of treatment techniques suitable for clinical work with these three clinical populations. Because children, unlike their adolescent and adult counterparts, have often not achieved full mastery of either spoken language or secondary process thinking, the use of the full adult range of verbalized communications is rarely possible for them (Lieberman, 1983). Thus doll play, puppetry, therapeutic games, modeling, mud and clay, painting and drawing, and other "play" techniques are used either alone or in conjunction with elicited narratives, which in turn involve either direct verbal exchange or communication made *per metaphor*.

## CHILDREN'S STORIES:
## AN OVERVIEW OF THE LITERATURE

In one form or another, stories and storytelling have constituted an important activity in psychodynamically oriented child therapy since the earliest clinical encounters with child patients in the first two decades of the twentieth century, although a review of the early child psychotherapy literature reveals relatively few instances in which storytelling is used systematically and independently of other psychotherapeutic techniques. Despite the relatively infrequent reports of techniques that made prominent use of stories and storytelling before the mid-1960s, the value of stories in both treatment and evaluation was recognized quite early. Indeed, it was almost nine decades ago that pioneering child psychoanalyst H. von Hug-Hellmuth (Hug-Hellmuth, 1913, 1921; Gardner, 1993) first suggested that children's projective stories and other fantasy play might provide the child analyst with dynamically meaningful information about a child's characteristic conflicts and adaptations. J. Conn (1939, 1941, 1948) and J. Solomon (1938, 1940, 1951) were among the first clinicians to experiment with children's stories both as projective media and as a technique in child psychotherapy; both are credited with early contributions to this literature (Gardner, 1993).

Louise Despert and her associate, H. W. Potter, reported in 1936 on a study undertaken to evaluate the story as a means of investigating psychiatric problems in children. Their subjects were twenty-two institutionalized children ranging in age from four to thirteen years. Although their research was not methodologically rigorous, Despert and Potter offered several conclusions based upon the impressionistic evidence they amassed:

- The story is a form of verbalized fantasy through which the child may reveal his or her inner drives and conflicts.
- A recurring theme generally indicates the principal concern or conflict, which in turn may be corroborated with other clinical evidence (e.g., dream material).

- Anxiety, guilt, wish-fulfillment, and aggressiveness are the primary trends expressed.
- The use of stories appears to be most valuable when the child determines the subject matter of his or her own story.
- The story can be used as both a therapeutic and an evaluation device.

Often, stories have been elicited by a child therapist in conjunction with particular therapeutic media or activities, such as puppetry (Bender and Woltmann, 1936; Hawkey, 1951; Woltmann, 1940, 1951), finger painting (Arlow and Kadis, 1946), drawing and watercolor painting (Rambert, 1949), costume play (Marcus, 1966); and clay modeling (Woltmann, 1950). Doll play (Millar, 1974) has also proved to be a rich source of stories and fantasies.

Some writers, among them L. Gondor (1957), have taken the position that the selection of a mode for communicating fantasies should depend on the child's own preference, necessitating the therapist's motivation and ingenuity in assisting the child to discover the best means of expression for such fantasies. Gondor illustrated this process with a clinical example involving a withdrawn ten-year-old patient who had difficulty with direct verbal communication but was able to express herself through the medium of a story, which was dictated to the therapist in weekly installments.

In fact, most techniques utilized in child psychotherapy have been designed to elicit fantasies, and not necessarily stories. Contemporary exponents of the

Kleinian school of play therapy might conceivably object to a technique requiring the child to produce an autogenic story, on the grounds that it imposes an unnecessary structure on the flow of material from the unconscious or that it restricts expression to the level of verbal communication. Phenomenologically speaking, however, such a story may be thought of as possessing an intermediate level of organization "somewhere between the more fluid primary process-like ideational activity of free association, and the more orderly, secondary process thinking of logical, conscious syntactical communication" (Kritzberg, 1975, p. 92). In other words, the autogenic story, though perhaps restricted to the domain of expressive language, does appear to provide reasonably direct access to a child's fantasy life, as do other techniques of play. One may even view the mandate to verbalize these fantasies in story form as a potential means of *enhancing* dynamic communication rather than diluting, masking, or distorting it. In one classic investigation of children's verbalized fantasies, eliciting an autogenic communication is described as comparable to eliciting a "dream on demand" (Pitcher and Prelinger, 1963).

Storytelling and story materials are sometimes associated with highly specialized procedures used in the psychotherapeutic treatment of children. One such procedure is *psychodrama*, in which children are called upon to utilize sociodramatic play in order to achieve insight into their behavior and to enable them to learn other, more appropriate roles for meeting the challenge of different interpersonal situations (Dreikurs, 1975; Starr, 1977). Another is the *structured therapeutic game method of child analytic psychotherapy* (Kritzberg, 1971, 1975), a method that combines stimulus-based (as opposed to autogenic) storytelling with two therapeutic games: The first (TISKIT, or Therapeutic Imaginative Storytelling Kit), designed for pre-literate children, contains iconic objects; the second (TASKIT, or Tell-A-Story-Kit), designed for school-age children, contains word-cards. The *mutual storytelling technique*, originally conceived as a reciprocal storytelling procedure (Gardner, 1977), was the earliest effort to formalize the use of children's autogenic stories. More recently, it has been combined with a variety of card and board games (Gardner, 1993). The *creative characters technique* (Brooks, 1981, 1993) is an interesting amalgam of N. Kritzberg's *structured therapeutic game method* and R. Gardner's *mutual storytelling technique;* more collaborative than reciprocal, it puts considerable focus on the strengthening of cognitive skills and various ego functions (e.g., anxiety-binding, promotion of mastery and competence).

The therapist's collaborative participation in the co-construction of children's stories has been used to clinical advantage by others. One example is J. Liebowitz's (1972) study of a severely disturbed seven-year-old whose use of storytelling was less a means of communication than a way of holding onto his relationship with the therapist. This child's stories had no plot or meaning—only characters with no apparent relationship to each other. Puppets and graphics materials were freely used to assist in the continuing therapeutic work with the child, and the therapist participated quite directly in altering or adding material to his autogenic stories. M. Robertson and F. Barford (1970) found therapist-constructed stories to be useful in therapeutic work with a chronically ill child hospitalized with respiratory failure. The stories were composed on a daily basis and incorporated not only the child's view of his life within the hospital but also the therapeutic team's perspective. The authors believed that the stories read to this child ultimately equipped him to involve himself "both psychologically and physiologically in the world beyond the hospital," culminating in his separation from the respirator and his eventual discharge (1970, p. 106). Additional modifications and applications of the basic reciprocal storytelling technique have been described by other authors as well (e.g., Claman, 1980; Gabel, 1984; Kestenbaum, 1985; Davis, 1986; Lawson, 1987).

## WHAT IS RECIPROCAL STORYTELLING?

The use of allegories, fables, parables, myths, and legends in the intergenerational transmission of important values and moral precepts has been traced to virtually every culture since the beginning of recorded history, underscoring the effectiveness of storytelling as a mode of communication with the young. Developmental psychology also tells us that children experience themselves from an early age "through the symbols they use to apprehend, encode, change, and describe experience," and that self-composed stories may serve as the "most essential symbolic process" for reflecting on and describing such experiences (Engel, 1999, p. 185).

*Reciprocal storytelling* was specifically designed as a means of both eliciting children's self-composed or autogenic stories and providing a therapeutic response to them in the context of psychoanalytic child psychotherapy. Compared to the dreams and free associations of adult patients, such stories and fantasy productions may indeed be less subject to the processes of censorship and distortion, and to other influences that obscure or disguise dynamic meaning. Autogenic stories, which of course are projective in nature, provide children with an opportunity to give expression to disturbing wishes, fears, and defensive adaptations in a "safe," though largely unconscious, metaphorical form. Because such stories are composed without specific thematic direction or guidance from the therapist or the use of storytelling "props," they are far more likely to represent faithfully the children's concerns, conflicts, and resolutions than are stories linked either to specific play materials or to themes suggested by the therapist.

The technique of reciprocal storytelling calls for the child's creation of an imaginary story with make-believe characters. The story must be original and there must be a beginning, some development, and an ending; sometimes, but not necessarily, a lesson or moral can be appended. The therapist then discerns the dynamic meaning of the story and responds within the story metaphor with a therapeutic version of his or her own. The responding story provides healthier, relatively conflict-free alternatives to the child's original conflict-laden solutions (Gardner, 1993).

One distinct advantage to the technique of reciprocal storytelling is the manner in which it shapes the patient-therapist discourse. Without creating a rigid structure that is inimical to both the clinical process and the basic objectives of sound psychodynamic treatment, the stories enhance the therapist's ability to apprehend and decode important primary process communications; at the same time, they offer a natural vehicle for therapeutic responses. The reciprocal storytelling process thus establishes an intersubjective discourse that can be maintained throughout treatment and serve as an undeniably powerful therapeutic tool for the child clinician.

## When Is Reciprocal Storytelling Useful and with Which Patients?

Storytelling procedures can be used selectively with children as young as three and as old as fifteen years, although the most effective age range seems to be school age to early adolescence (roughly five to twelve years). Reciprocal storytelling, in particular, appears to be therapeutically effective across a wide spectrum of childhood problems and emotional disorders: phobias, anxiety disorders, depression, obsessive-compulsive problems; chronic depletion states, selfobject disorders, and difficulty in the regulation of self-esteem; sequelae of emotional neglect and physical and/or sexual abuse. It is especially helpful in work with children of divorce and those suffering from other environmental crises (e.g., loss of a parent or sibling, life-threatening illness of a close family member). In addition, children who have experienced trauma—that is, in cases where a massive paralysis of ego functions has occurred—may be receptive to the use of such story communications *per metaphor*. Therapists may also find reciprocal storytelling a useful adjunct in their clinical work with children suffering from chronic or life-threatening illnesses, or with those who have developmental disabilities. Even schizoid children, or those with nascent borderline personality disorders, may be good candidates for reciprocal storytelling.

Storytelling also seems to work well with resistant children. It may, in fact, provide the therapist with a vehicle for circumnavigating or surmounting initial resistance and establishing a basic working alliance despite the children's disinclination to reveal much of themselves in more direct verbal discourse or even through other play activities. Owing to the fact that stories are "make-believe," children seem reassured that they are not actually revealing anything of great import about themselves. So far as they are concerned, any disturbing wishes, conflicts, secrets, and the like are safely obscured from view. Precisely—and paradoxically—because the story is ostensibly about *someone else*, it permits the *most* important unconscious conflicts and disturbing fantasies, as well as other closely guarded or otherwise hidden parts of the self, to emerge in a disguised though decodable form.

On the other hand, storytelling isn't for everyone; nor is it invariably effective even for the same patient at different points in the treatment process. Certain children with developmental disabilities may be incapable of the minimal cognitive organization required for even the most elementary story. Others whose expressive language is compromised by developmental or organic factors may prefer play activities that do not highlight spoken language. Still others may enjoy the reciprocal storytelling process early in the treatment relationship but later express a preference for alternative play activities. This is especially true over long courses of treatment that begin in pre-adolescence. In such instances, the child's increasing developmental sophistication makes storytelling as well as other play activities seem infantilizing. Indeed, like any other technique in the child psychotherapist's repertoire, storytelling should be deployed with sensitivity and in accord with a particular child's preferences.

It is not essential for a child to be highly verbal in order for such techniques to be used successfully. Even a short, three-line story from a very young or self-conscious child may prove quite revealing, in much the same way that adult patients' dream "fragments" often seem to be. Furthermore, when children express little confidence in their ability to compose a make-believe story, the therapist may suggest the use of a pictorial adjunct to the storytelling procedure to help them "get started." D. W. Winnicott's (1971) *squiggle* technique is ideally suited for such occasions, inasmuch as it provides a natural lead-in to story making without suggesting specific themes or story-content to the child.

The squiggle technique calls for the clinician and child to take turns drawing "squiggly" lines and completing each other's squiggle drawings. The squiggle is made with one's eyes closed, although the other subject always completes the drawing with his or her eyes open. Winnicott characteristically used the squiggle content as a springboard for analytic investigation;

he did not always work within the metaphor of the drawing in the discussions that followed, nor did he ask the child to use the picture to compose an original story, although some of his subjects did this spontaneously.

When a story is the goal, however, it should always be based on the child's completed drawing rather than on the therapist's. The same ground rules apply: The story must be original, the characters must be imaginary, and there must be a beginning, some development of the story, and an ending. I don't require a moral or lesson since I don't believe this to be absolutely essential, but I will sometimes suggest that one be included. Years of personal observation confirm that even children who at first claim to be poor storytellers or unable to "think of one" to tell will suddenly launch into a story without any further prompting. In these instances, the process of creating a drawing from the squiggle somehow liberates preconscious fantasies and their accompanying affects in such children. In fact, some children prefer to base their stories on such drawings, even though they may already have demonstrated an ability to compose their stories independently of this technique. The therapist is well advised to honor the child's wish to combine these two media and, indeed, may be rewarded for doing so with particularly fertile results.

### Eliciting the Child's Story

Because storytelling is for most children a mode of narrative interchange that is both experience-near and entertaining, they are typically more than pleased to provide an autogenic story at the clinician's request. Inasmuch as original stories are a more accurate measure of the child's issues, conflicts, and adaptations, the clinician may wish to emphasize that telling *made-up* stories is more fun than simply repeating something one has seen on a children's show or a video. (Although there is undoubtedly always some contamination of the content from exposure to movies, videos, and television, it is generally not pronounced.) Most children at six or seven years of age are able to provide reasonably well-integrated stories without a specific injunction to include a beginning, a middle, and an end. The use of a tape recorder frequently serves to enhance the children's storytelling, allowing them the narcissistic satisfaction of hearing their own voice played back. And at least one author has suggested that the storytelling process can be "framed" as a television show, in which the therapist serves as the interviewer/moderator and the child is introduced as a "special guest" (Gardner, 1977). Such an approach may be quite appealing to some children and, in any event, establishes a somewhat more natural linkage with audio or videotape. Certain children, however, are resistant to the idea of audio recording or videotaping their stories and may experience such technology as intrusive or anxiety-generating. The recording of stories and perhaps even the therapist's note taking may be contraindicated with these children or with others who exhibit paranoid ideation or fears.

Occasionally, a child will ask the therapist to construct a story collaboratively. Although the likelihood of the therapist's influence over story theme and content is undoubtedly increased in such instances, there are ways to minimize this effect; one might, for example, consent to help with the introduction though not with the rest of the story. Certain children, especially those who lack self-confidence, or who are extremely anxious or perhaps decompensation-prone, may require this parameter until they are sufficiently self-assured to create a story without the therapist's active collaboration.

### The Lesson or Moral

For many, a well-told children's story is one that ends with a moral or lesson—certainly a time-honored and integral feature of numerous cautionary tales, fables, fairy tales, and other kinds of stories. The lesson or moral is particularly helpful, too, because it identifies for the listener what the story is intended to teach. Among younger listeners less able to accomplish this task without some assistance, a carefully articulated lesson or moral may make the story both more memorable and more meaningful.

Although it is true that asking the child to draw a lesson or moral at the conclusion of an *autogenic* story (Gardner, 1977, 1993) may sometimes enable the therapist to select the most salient theme or clarify the meaning of ambiguous story content, that lesson or moral will not always be especially well matched to story theme or content. In fact, it may be chosen not for reasons having any obvious connection to its dynamic meaning but, rather, because the child knows a particular proverb and tosses it in as a way of pleasing the therapist. (Instead of specifically requesting a moral from a younger child, the therapist may find it more helpful to ask "what the story teaches.") Even those therapists who do not believe that doing without a moral from the child results in a significant loss of data may wish to include a moral or lesson at the conclusion of their responding story. In such cases the moral or lesson creates an additional opportunity for the therapist to demonstrate alternative strategies or new ways of thinking about problems that enhance the child's adaptive evolution of his or her narrative account.[1]

## Post-story Discussion

It is often beneficial to explore the child's understanding of the stories at the conclusion of storytelling. This practice permits the therapist to test the child's awareness of particular story elements that may differ between the two story versions. It can also serve as a natural segue to other play activities. And at times, post-story inquiry can provide a point of de-

---

[1]Note, however, that in the clinical examples that follow, some of the children assigned titles to their stories, some supplied morals, some furnished both, and others did neither. It may be a measure of the elasticity of this technique that the child's disinclination to title a story or include a lesson or moral rarely has a negative consequence for the therapeutic discourse. An analogy can be drawn to the use of dreams in the psychotherapy of adults, whereby the raw data—the dream content and dreamer's associations—are far more valuable than the need for imposing an invariant set of organizing principles to aid in their interpretation. In effect, then, the therapist works with the child's stories in the form that the child is most comfortable with and capable of supplying.

parture for discussing the child's conflicted feelings, fantasies, or thematically relevant recent experiences. Note, however, that although therapists do not generally find it problematic to use the stories as a springboard for discussion, perhaps even to suggest a certain similarity between some feature of the story and a recent experience of the child, direct interpretation is best avoided.

## THE THERAPIST'S ROLE IN THE STORYTELLING PROCESS

The therapist's role in using stories is not appreciably different than it would be for any other activity in the therapeutic playroom. Listening carefully while remaining empathically attuned, discerning meaning in the child's play and verbalizations, and conveying such understanding in a form that the child can grasp and ultimately internalize—all of these capacities apply equally to the storytelling process.

Composing make-believe stories—like drawing, painting, or clay modeling—involves the child's creative imagination. The story is, in this sense, a creative product that the child has shared with the therapist. It should also be humbling. No matter how skilled or clever the therapist's response to this creation of the patient's, the response must *always* be based on the *child's* material. Children recognize this connection right away and may even comment that the therapist's story sounds very much like their own (a creative debt that the therapist should graciously acknowledge).

As suggested earlier, it is important for the integrity of the storytelling process that such creative products not be approached via direct interpretation (except in highly unusual circumstances, as discussed in Chapter 2). In other words, the therapist should respond *within the child's story-metaphor* rather than interpreting story themes, conflicts, or other content to the child. When the therapist's immediate response to the child's story is made outside the metaphor, not only are the "ground rules" violated and the therapist's trustworthiness called into question, but the child may become convinced that the therapist has special extrasensory abilities.

Nevertheless, it can be quite useful to engage in a sort of post-story dialogue in which the therapist seeks to clarify ambiguous elements of the child's story and also to establish parallels between the story characters or themes and experiences or issues in the child's life. Such discussion can occur immediately, later within the same session in connection with a different play activity, or even in a subsequent session.

Due to the reciprocal nature of this play technique, the child will expect to hear a therapeutic response to his or her story. Although it is clinically optimal for the therapist to offer a story-response within a few minutes of the conclusion of the child's presentation, this is not always possible. Sometimes, the content of the child's story will be ambiguous; at other times, the clinician, whether due to fatigue or perhaps a countertransference reaction, will simply be unable to grasp the meaning of a given story. Under such circumstances, the therapist might wish to consider three alternatives:

1. After the therapist explains that he or she is unable to tell a responding story right away, therapist and patient engage in a different activity and return to the storytelling at a later point in the treatment hour. Because the dynamic meaning of a child's story is often played out in other activities during the session, the therapist will have additional opportunities to apprehend whatever had proven elusive about the child's story earlier in the session.

2. Another technique involves asking the child to create a "commercial" (Gardner, 1977), the premise being twofold: (a) It permits the therapist to "stall for time," providing a few precious minutes to pore over the child's text in a search for meaning; and (b) whatever salient dynamic issues are contained in the autogenic story are also presumed to be present in the "commercial." This technique has proven beneficial at times, although nearly as often the child seems to view it as an open invitation to make undisguised use of actual television commercials. In consequence, it may frequently be more a source of distraction than a means of enhancing the therapist's understanding of the child's narrative.

3. A third solution is to admit defeat and not attempt a therapeutic response, at least within

that particular therapy hour. In this instance, the therapist may offer a simple apology for being unable to tell a good story in response to the child's offering. Important dynamic themes are, after all, likely to resurface in subsequent interviews. The frank admission of inability to come up with a story-response despite the desire to do so typically elicits a sympathetic reaction; it may even pave the way for less inherently ambiguous revelations from the child. Indeed, those children locked in competitive struggle with the therapist may welcome such an admission as confirmation of a successful sortie against the enemy. This development can be viewed as an opportunity to comment on the obvious pleasure the child appears to have derived from outwitting the therapist. Should the comment prove evocative for the child, the therapist may then wish to explore the transference meaning of such competitive behavior in further dialogue.

Also, there are times, typically near the end of a successful course of therapy, when the therapist finds it difficult to improve upon a child's story, in which case common sense dictates that the therapist not even try. Earlier in the course of therapy, too, the repertoire of strategies a child deploys to resolve conflict may include both maladaptive or conflict-laden elements as well as somewhat more adaptive solutions *in statu nascendi*. The latter, of course, should always be validated and supported in the therapist's story-responses. When, at a later point in treatment, these nascent adaptive solutions are more fully evolved and have supplanted less adaptive strategies, the therapist can simply explain that the child's story is so well told that it can stand fully on its own. This situation is golden: In fact, it is a goal of the whole treatment process that the child internalize new and increasingly adaptive strategies for solving conflicts, develop new capacities for emotional growth, and, in so doing, make the therapy and the therapist superfluous. Insofar as highly adaptive, well-told stories serve as evidence that the child has "brought it all together," they provide reassuring confirmation of his or her readiness to consider termination of therapy.[2] (See the case of Roberta in Chapter 4.)

## WHAT ARE THE MOST IMPORTANT COMPONENTS OF CHILDREN'S STORIES?

In every story, the child therapist should strive to identify the dynamic theme or issue; the object relations scenario and key self and object representations; the affective tone of the story; paralinguistic, visual, and kinesic cues; and, finally, the child's defensive behaviors, discrete defenses, defensive strategies, and conflict-free solutions.

---

[2]Of course, there are many other important indices for assessing a child's readiness to terminate, among them amelioration of the presenting symptoms, the reports of parents and teachers, the therapist's general observations, and the child's subjective report.

- *The dynamic theme or issue.* What is the most salient issue, theme, or focal conflict appearing in the child's story? Childhood is filled with a range of normative problems and conflicts even when it is not disrupted by environmental crises or pathology. Various needs predominate at different phases of psychosocial and psychosexual development; they encompass everything from preschoolers' requirements for affirmation of their normal exhibitionism to the struggles of adolescents to combat the regressive pull of the nuclear family in an effort to extend their radius of social relationships. Typical focal conflicts revealed in the stories of children might be *hostility versus guilt*, the wish for *intimacy versus fear of engulfment*, the wish to be *assertive versus fear of criticism*, or the desire for *autonomy versus fear of abandonment/rejection*.
- *The object relations scenario and self and object representations.* Children's stories sometimes portray a unique object relational experience derived from important, affectively charged early encounters with parents, siblings, and others. Such an experience may then serve as a lens through which all subsequent object relations may be understood. For example, a ten-year-old boy whose mother tended to be overprotective, as well as somewhat intolerant of his efforts to achieve psychological autonomy, told stories in which a small, rather helpless character (usually depicted as a small animal) was dominated by a larger

and more powerful character. Every autonomous effort of the smaller character was somehow thwarted or undermined by the larger one, who, like the patient's mother, tended to discourage the smaller character from venturing out, being more assertive, and so forth. Even when such an object relational scenario cannot reliably be identified, it is always useful to determine which character(s) may represent the storyteller and which character(s) appear to represent other important figures in the child's life (e.g., parents, siblings, or the therapist).

- *The affective tone of the story.* Another important element in a child's autogenic story is affective or hedonic tone. Is the story told with anticipatory pleasure, vigor, and enthusiasm? Or is it narrated in a monotone, perhaps with a hint of dysphoria? Does the child sound mildly annoyed, angry, hurt, frustrated, anxious, agitated, fatigued, or confused? Does the affective tone match the feelings of the story characters, the action, or the thematic content? Does the child's affect remain invariant throughout, or does it shift mildly or even markedly? At times, a child's identification with a particular story character becomes clear only when the therapist realizes that the *storyteller's* affects are changing each time that character is described or speaks, in a manner somewhat analogous to the use of *leitmotif* in Wagnerian opera.

- *Paralinguistic, visual, and kinesic cues.* The narration of stories is usually accompanied by a variety of sublingual utterances, distinctive facial expressions, and other, sometimes quite revealing bodily movements. Although such cues are generally consonant with the content of the story and simply serve to "drive home" particular themes or story action, they will occasionally be rather asynchronous or poorly matched with story content and theme. For instance, a very depressed nine-year-old girl, whose father abandoned the family, had quite a fanciful imagination. Her stories often had themes involving larger-than-life characters who embarked on high adventures in exotic locales. As she told these stories, however, her manner was remarkable for its *economy* of movement, and she looked and sounded depressed, her demeanor at striking variance with the imaginative tales she told.

- *The child's defensive behaviors, discrete defenses, defensive strategies, and conflict-free solutions.* According to a classic research investigation of normal two- to five-year-olds (Pitcher and Prelinger, 1963), autogenic stories, like dreams, contain compromise solutions to conflict. In stories, children struggle with unconscious wishes (generally of a disturbing libidinal or aggressive nature) that strive for direct expression or discharge. These wishes activate the synthetic function of the ego, which recognizes the danger of direct expression or fulfillment of the disturbing wish and seeks to disguise it, constructing a story that, according to these authors, both assuages the superego and appears to conform to essential standards of realism and social acceptability. Ultimately, the autogenic story, in a manner analogous to the dream, attempts to resolve the conflict activated by the disturbing wish through whatever means are readily available to the ego. Among these are defensive behaviors in very young children (e.g., transformation of affect), discrete defenses (e.g., denial, undoing, isolation, or withdrawal), and wishes used defensively (e.g., hostility directed against the self, defensive intimacy, or defensive assertion). Relatively conflict-free adaptive strategies emerge as the child acquires more capacity for self-observation and insight, usually during the latter phases of treatment.

## WHICH THEORETICAL FRAMEWORKS ARE COMPATIBLE WITH RECIPROCAL STORYTELLING?

Although reciprocal storytelling is compatible with any of the major systems used in the practice of psychoanalytic child psychotherapy, the clinical illustrations provided in the examples throughout this book are guided by two basic frameworks: (1) ego psychology informed by object relations theory and (2) the psychology of the self. *Ego psychology* is principally concerned with the ego and its functions, and presumes the existence of intrapsychic conflict, which is mediated by the defenses as well as by various strategies and mechanisms of adaptation. It is rooted in the structural hypothesis of classical Freudian theory, although ego psychology takes greater account of the role of the environment than does classical psychoanalysis. The *psychology of the self* is a newer psychoanalytic psychology based on the contributions of Heinz Kohut (1977, 1984). In contrast to the conflict basis of ego psychology, self psychology is a deficit-based psychology, focusing far more on the availability of certain kinds of psychological supplies thought to be necessary for the evolution of a vital and harmonious or *cohesive self*.[3]

What follows introduces and illustrates the reciprocal storytelling process.

---

[3]Kohut and his followers believed that such developmental supplies are made available through three major kinds of relational configurations, termed *selfobject relationships*, so named because they refer to a particular kind of relationship in which the object is actually experienced as an extension of the self, without psychological differentiation. The three selfobject experiences are *mirroring, idealizing,* and *partnering.* Each corresponds to a particular domain of self experience: Mirroring experiences are associated with an intrapsychic structure known as the *grandiose-exhibitionistic self*, reflecting the need for approval, interest, and affirmation; idealizing experiences, with the *idealized parent imago*, reflecting the developmental need for closeness and support from an (omnipotent) and idealized other; and partnering experiences, with the *alter ego*, reflecting the need for contact with others who are felt to bear an essential likeness to the self. Collectively, these three domains

## THE CASE OF TONY

Eleven-year-old Tony, attractive if somewhat overweight, was originally referred for treatment because of poor academic performance and behavioral problems at home. His mother anxiously described their relationship as highly conflicted and admitted in a rush of words to feeling both helpless and exasperated in her attempt to parent him. Although Tony typically did not openly challenge her authority, he often subverted, ignored, or sabotaged her efforts; that pattern, and in particular its impact on his two younger siblings, had become a source of growing concern. Tony's almost characterological tendency to procrastinate had negative ramifications for his performance in school and especially irritated his mother. His father, an academician and research scientist, often worked long hours at his lab and traveled extensively to lecture at scientific conferences; he was, and always had been, much less involved with Tony than she.

Tony's mother's portrait of her son's infancy and early childhood contrasted markedly with the presenting picture: She remembered him as an active, happy toddler who smiled at strangers and was captured on home video repeatedly and gleefully running circles around his tired mother—but she now complained about his inactivity, passivity, and dislike of

---

are called the *tri-polar* self, and each is also linked to a particular transference configuration. Self psychology places great emphasis on the role of empathy in human development, imputing a special significance to traumatic breaches or disruptions in empathic attunement between self and selfobject. Not only the original, thwarted selfobject needs but also the ensuing empathic ruptures are often recapitulated in the child's evolving transference relationship.

doing physical things. Tony had been a poor eater, and because he seemed to gain weight so slowly, his mother switched from breast milk to formula and began to force-feed him early on, although she admitted this was partly in response to pressure from her husband's extended family. By age two, Tony had become "a better eater"; but an early and significant pattern had clearly been forged in the relationship between mother and son.

Although later developmental milestones were unremarkable, Tony did not react well to the birth of his two siblings. His brother was born when Tony was twenty-two months old, and a sister came along some three years later. According to his mother, Tony's problems at home often seemed connected to his dislike and jealousy of David and, to a lesser degree, Patty. By sixth grade, Tony's school performance had deteriorated so markedly that consideration was being given to either special classroom placement or grade retention. Because subsequent testing revealed Tony to be a very bright youngster whose intelligence clearly exceeded the cognitive and intellectual requirements of the work he was being asked to do, such solutions didn't seem particularly viable and, therefore, were dismissed.

Tony was a very agreeable patient and appeared to enjoy a number of activities in the playroom, though in his rather quiet and understated way. One of these playroom pursuits was reciprocal storytelling, an activity in which we engaged to very good effect over the entire course of his sixteen-month-long therapy. At the time that Tony told me the following story, approximately nine months into therapy, we had been discussing the anger and jealousy he felt toward his younger brother. Tony had made some progress in his school performance and there was moderate improvement in his relation-

ship with his mother, but the rivalry with his younger siblings
continued to be a problem.

---

## TONY'S STORY

Once upon a time there was a fireplace, but it hadn't
been used in a long time. These people who lived there
were going to knock it down in order to put in a heating
system. Well, this builder came by and said to them,
"Don't knock it down. I'll take it and put it in my
house." Except he really didn't use it much. Well, one
day, he was sitting by it, and it cracked, and the bricks
started to fall. It was falling apart. He tried to fix it, but
it just fell apart again. Finally, he sold it to some people
who turned it into a new fireplace, one that was worth
more money than the old fireplace.
*Moral: Just because things are old doesn't mean they're worth
a lot of money.*

## ANALYSIS

Nowhere among Tony's remarks were the twin themes
of sibling jealousy and narcissistic injury more
poignantly expressed than in this story, although they
were repeatedly reprised in Tony's other stories and
play activities. The way in which he chose to represent
himself here, as an old fireplace, makes for a densely
packed metaphor really quite ingenious in its economy of expression. It emblematizes at once his passivity, his seething anger, and his desire to "shine
brightly" before an admiring mother and father.

An old fireplace is scheduled for demolition, to be replaced by a newer, more modern heating system (Tony's younger siblings). Tony believes that the birth of his younger siblings has made him obsolete, like the old fireplace; not only does his mother seem endlessly preoccupied with the needs of his younger brother and sister, but his father is similarly unavailable, running laboratory experiments or away from home at professional conferences. Tony has suffered a series of narcissistic and oedipal defeats in relation to both siblings, although his "fall from grace" is more clearly connected to David's birth when Tony was not quite two. Although there is a certain degree of *secondary gain* to be extracted from his school-related problems and his conflicts with his siblings and his mother, the gratifications prove to be fleeting.

Interestingly, the "builder" in his story, who appears to have been introduced as a therapist-representative, seems at first quite genuinely interested in the fireplace. He prevails upon the house owners, the parent-representatives in this story, to permit him to take the fireplace home with him, thereby rescuing it. Sadly, however, the fireplace once again falls into disuse. The transference significance of this plot development is inescapable: The old fireplace is simply incapable of evoking any sustained interest, even from the well-meaning builder-therapist. Tony will eventually suffer the same sort of oedipal and narcissistic defeats with the therapist as he has experienced with his own parents.

In his story, the most prominent maladaptive solution the fireplace adopts is to shake itself apart.[4] Not even the builder is able to repair the fireplace, so he sells it to someone else, who proceeds to turn the old fireplace into a new one, enhancing its value in the process. The story's moral simply repeats the passive and masochistic solutions present in the story itself: Old things (fireplaces, older siblings) aren't worth very much to anyone and, sooner or later, will need to be replaced or rebuilt. In keeping with the helpless and passive voice that pervades the story, it seems almost futile to attempt to counteract this eventuality.

*[Based on this understanding, I responded with a story of my own, using many of the same story elements. But there are also critical differences.]*

---

THERAPIST'S RESPONSE

Once upon a time, there was a fireplace that used to be the center of attention. Then the people who owned it decided to create a new heating system. The fireplace became neglected, and no one sat by it anymore. One day, a builder saw that the fireplace wasn't doing well and suggested that the fireplace come to his shop so that he could repair it. Well, the fireplace worked better for a while, but then it started to fall apart again. The fireplace felt neglected and displaced by the heating system, and didn't even care anymore, although it didn't know why it wasn't working well.

---

[4]Although one might argue that this element represents the experience of disintegration anxiety, I am more inclined to view it as an example of self-directed hostility owing to Tony's relatively stable self-cohesiveness.

However, there were things about the fireplace that made it unique. First, it could burn logs, and the heating system couldn't. That meant that even if there was a power failure, the fireplace could always provide warmth to the family as long as they brought logs in from the outside. The fireplace was also unique in that it was really cozy on cold nights, and people liked to curl up next to it as long as its flame didn't burn too brightly. People actually seemed to enjoy spending time at the fireplace, but it is true that the heating system demanded more attention from the family at times.

Anyway, the builder told the fireplace that it needed to remember that it couldn't always provide all the heat for the house, but it certainly could sometimes. He also said that if the fireplace could control its flame better, then people would probably be more likely to want to sit near it. Sometimes, of course, it's important to burn brightly so that people know you're still there, as long as your sparks don't fly out of the fireplace (since that can upset or scare people). The fireplace found these ideas interesting, and agreed to try the builder's suggestions.

*Moral: If you're a fireplace and people neglect you, try doing these things: Remember that you have to share heating the house with the more modern heating system; try to control your flame so that people will want to sit by you; and, if you're feeling like people aren't paying enough attention to you, try burning brightly for a little while, but without making sparks fly since that upsets or even scares people.*

## Discussion

In my story-response, I attempted to address several interrelated story elements. First, while preserving the fireplace metaphor, I tried to confer a sense of agency on the fireplace. In effect, a fireplace doesn't have to be completely passive or helplessly dependent upon others all of the time, as the fireplace in Tony's story was. The fireplace can work with the builder in arriving at a better and more adaptive solution for its problems. Second, it is possible for a fireplace to use aggression constructively (heating up the room for the rest of the family), rather than for the purpose of acting out against others (letting sparks fly), or defensively (punishing itself by shaking apart). I believe that this idea, even after many months of therapy, remained a relatively novel one for Tony and was obviously a perspective he had yet to internalize fully. Finally, my builder counseled the fireplace to "burn brightly" as a way of vigorously announcing its needs, suggesting—aside from the issue of how aggression can be harnessed and used adaptively—that the fireplace deserves and is entitled to the appreciation of others. Others will admire its warmth and uniqueness, at least some of the time. By the same token, one cannot always be the center of attention; sometimes others will have the spotlight, and one must be tolerant and sufficiently flexible to sustain the corresponding narcissistic slights.

As he had countless times before, Tony participated in this storytelling exchange in a quiet, intently focused manner. He received my story-response with interest, although in our post-story discussions it was rarely possible to make direct connections between our narrative exchanges and his experiences outside of therapy. Tony would simply shrug, indicating that he had "made up a story" in accordance with the rules I had introduced in our very first session. In essence, the stories were "make believe," having nothing to do with him—a claim made relatively often by children when asked about the relationship of their stories to events or circumstances in their lives (Gardner, 1993). Nevertheless, Tony gradually became quite invested in his therapy. This wasn't always clear from his predictably low-key presentation during our treatment hours; however, he often arrived early for his sessions, and he became far more interactive as we neared the termination phase of his therapy (occasioned by a family move out of state). Although Tony's treatment ended prematurely, he had already begun to show considerable improvement in his academic performance, and his mother reported significant strides in his tolerance for his younger siblings as well as in his relationship with her.

## SUMMARY

Although stories and storytelling have long been utilized as a means of therapeutic communication with children, storytelling activities have generally not been formalized, usually occurring in conjunction with other therapeutic activities such as doll play, puppetry, or therapeutic board games. Storytelling, however, can be used to considerable therapeutic advantage when it involves autogenic content and occurs within a reciprocal exchange. In such a procedure, the therapist must identify the most salient dynamic issues or themes in the child's version, offering a therapeutic rendering of the child's story that preserves the basic theme, plot elements, and characters from the child's autogenic story. The therapist's story is intended to offer dynamic interpretations of the child's original version, *within the metaphor*. Such a procedure establishes safety in the therapeutic dialogue, permitting the child therapist to make important dynamic communications and to suggest increasingly adaptive alternatives for the resolution of conflict without educing the resistance that so often accompanies more direct interpretation of dynamic issues and intrapsychic conflicts.

Reciprocal storytelling is most valuable as a *technique* rather than a *method* of child treatment. Other playroom activities, including those traditionally associated with psychoanalytic child psychotherapy, are no less generative or useful; the process of child treatment can be enhanced by the addition of reciprocal exchanges *per metaphor*, however.

# CHAPTER 2

# Autogenic Stories, Projective Drawings, and the Clinical Assessment Process

Although stories and storytelling hold a time-honored role in *therapeutic* work with children, the elicitation of an autogenic (stimulus-independent) story for *diagnostic* purposes has not generally been advocated as a useful technique. Yet children's stories have long been recognized as important sources of information about intrapsychic structure, characteristic conflicts, and defensive adaptations. They can also provide information about disturbing wishes and fantasies, interpersonal relations, the development of the self, and other aspects of character.

Such *projective* instruments as the Roberts Apperception Test, Bellak's Children's Apperception Test (CAT), and Blum's Blacky Pictures have made use of pictorial stimuli suggesting various themes to elicit data from children in story form (Roberts, 1982; Blum, 1950; Bellak and Bellak, 1949). Although the projective story told in response to a pictorial stimulus is a valuable indicator of "the child's structure, defenses, and his dynamic way of reacting to, and handling his problems of growth" (Bellak, 1954, p. 149), it constitutes a clinical communication very different from the autogenic story.

The autogenic story has been described as the product of an interplay of forces phenomenologically similar to that of the dream (Pitcher and Prelinger, 1963):

> These forces consist on the one hand of unconscious wishes striving for expression and fulfillment, and on the other of forces aiming to disguise these wishes and to produce a story that is reasonably conforming to standards of realism and social acceptability. Each story thus represents a compromise solution to a conflict. (pp. 216–117)

Although it has been suggested that the first story a child tells in treatment  receive a therapeutic response (Gardner, 1977), there are drawbacks to the use of what is essentially a therapeutic technique for diagnostic purposes. The recommendation rests on the questionable assumption that reciprocal storytelling can function effectively prior to the formation of even a rudimentary therapeutic alliance and the establishment of an intersubjective discourse, and in spite of the fact that "one may not know enough about a child to ascertain the psychodynamics of his first story" (p. 33)—thereby adding to the difficulty of creating a meaningful story in response.

But in the assessment phase, the objective is to learn about the nature of the child's conflicts, not to respond therapeutically.[1] Although a sort of nonspecific "treatment" often begins with the initial diagnostic interview—if only in consequence of the clinician's empathic attention to the child—the distinction between assessment and treatment needs to be maintained. Pragmatically, the therapist is unlikely to have enough clinical data to construct a meaningful response. Moreover, a child's first autogenic story is a unique clinical communication, one that serves as a sort of narrative statement of the child's nuclear conflict, however oblique and metaphorical. The revelation of the child's deepest struggles in this form is closely paralleled in the adult patient's first dream, which often signifies the particular dynamic issue of greatest concern to the dreamer (Fromm-Reichmann, 1950). Such material can be imbued with personal meanings in a manner unsurpassed by other forms of communication. Indeed, repeated observations have

---

[1]Of course, dynamically oriented clinical assessment of children, when meaningfully undertaken as a separate, preliminary phase preceding treatment, involves the integration of an extensive body of information derived from various sources, including the child, his or her parents, teachers, and other collaterals. Clinical impressionistic data based on interaction with both parents and the child as well as a thorough history taking with detailed information on the developmental milestones are regarded as essential. Other important components include the history of the presenting complaint, intercurrent environmental variables, development of the ego and its overall functioning, superego development, development of the self, libidinal and aggressive drive development, and the child's repertoire of defensive and adaptive strategies for handling conflict.

confirmed that certain kinds of clinical material can be very near the surface in early interviews, only to become inaccessible once treatment is under way.

## AUTOGENIC STORIES AND THE DIAGNOSTIC PROCESS

The story in most instances should not be elicited until midway through the initial diagnostic interview, or until the clinician feels that he or she has achieved some measure of rapport with the child. Children who express curiosity as to the clinician's reasons for requesting a story from them can be told that stories, like pictures and other play activities, help the clinician to better understand the nature of their problems and ways in which they can be helped to solve them. The self-conscious or shy child may be assisted in starting the story ("Once upon a time, there was a . . . "), although the clinician must be especially careful not to suggest content to the child. The child's pleasure in listening to the clinician's responses is, of course, absent when the story is used for diagnostic purposes and there is no responding story. However, most children will cooperate with the clinician's request for one or two such stories, much as they would with a request for a *house-tree-person* drawing or with other fundamentally (nonreciprocal) diagnostic procedures.

The seven case vignettes that follow are all drawn from the diagnostic phase. Although each involves a distinctive clinical issue, they collectively illustrate the range of information that can be extrapolated from a child's first autogenic story.

## THE CASE OF SEAN

When Sean was five, his natural parents relinquished custody in order to have him placed in a foster home. It is probably an understatement to describe his relationships by that time with both of them, particularly his mother, as malignant. Although Sean was completely out of control, destroying furniture and willfully urinating on the carpet and walls, the intensity of his hatred was equaled by theirs; they urgently requested foster placement in the interest of their survival and his.

Probably not incidentally, Sean had been afflicted with a relatively rare neonatal condition known as pyloric stenosis, whereby a malformation of the valve connecting the pylorus to the duodenum prevents babies from digesting milk. Its most common symptom is a rather dramatic one, projectile vomiting. In Sean's case, owing to a combination of professional oversight and maternal denial, this serious condition went undiagnosed for a period of some six weeks, during which his mother's frustration in feeding him developed into a deep sense of maternal inadequacy and incompetence; both were most certainly mirrored in the disturbed mother-infant relationship that followed. Perhaps it is no exaggeration to speculate that their early, painful experience became a sort of template repeatedly and unconsciously applied to later experiences. Regardless, Sean was a difficult baby whose physical problems and temperament brought little joy to his parents.

Sean was by now eleven years old. He had spent the last half of his life being shuffled from one placement to another. At the time I started working with him, he was a co-resident in a privately operated group home staffed by a couple in their sixties who had been hired to serve as "treatment parents" for the eight or nine children in their care. A bright child with a fanciful imagination, Sean already demonstrated a significant degree of emotional disturbance. He had tremendous difficulty in negotiating interpersonal relationships, often losing his temper with other children, teachers, or the adult staff at the group home. He was quite impulsive; his moods were unpredictable and often vacillated between extremes, further compromising his ability to maintain control over powerful emotions that often threatened to overwhelm him.

Sean's moodiness and impulsiveness, combined with his difficulty in exercising good judgment, evoked Freud's metaphor of the id as a riderless horse (Freud, 1923)—a bundle of impulses and disturbing wishes and fantasies continually threatening to erupt without the steadying influence of the ego. Sean was largely incapable of controlling the horse and reining in his powerful emotions, at least without assistance in the form of intercession from others. When his history of marked developmental lags, evident failure to attain object or self constancy, and other deviations and abnormalities was integrated with the emergent clinical picture, the result strongly suggested a nascent borderline personality organization.

During our initial meeting, Sean seemed somewhat intrigued by my request that he "make up" a story, and he produced the first of some sixty stories he was to tell over nine months of twice-weekly treatments. This is what he presented, in dark, almost somber tones:

---

SEAN'S STORY

Once upon a time there was a cat who lived in a lost alley, and he was all alone. He had no friends. He would catch rats in a trash can and eat them, but he would still feel lonely. One day, he was out on a walk feeling grumpy as usual, and lonely, and kind of low-headed. He walked out and all of a sudden he heard a purr. It was another cat, exactly like him. Same breed, same everything, same eyes, same looks. So they decided to get together and play tricks on people, and they would go and knock on a door. They would scratch on the door to get the people's attention, and then the people would keep them. And then one cat had a favorite sport of clawing people. So, he went scratching on the door, the people kept him and then they sent him to the Humane Society. They thought he was kinda playful, kinda scratchy, but kinda playful. That night the (first) cat snuck out and the other cat came in. The next morning the people were talking about how scratchy he is and that they might have to send him to the Humane Society. *[When asked at this juncture to identify the two cats, Sean said Cat Number 1 is the scratchy cat and Cat Number 2 plays with yarn.]* So all of a sudden Cat Number 2 snuck in. He looked like he was kinda lonely or something, so the people were thinking that maybe they would send him to someone who might want him. So that morning—the mother knits and she dropped some yarn—the cat started playing with the yarn, so she grabbed the cat and she goes, "The cat doesn't scratch, the cat doesn't scratch!" The cat didn't scratch her. So all was well, you know. They thought, "Oh, wow! Our cat doesn't scratch anymore." So they got their friends over that night, and they (the friends) saw the cat. "Wow, is he nice," they said, and then they got done playing with the cat. That night, while they were asleep the other cat (Cat Number 1) came in. And he started scratching at the covers and everything. Well, they decided that there

were two cats, or else he has two personalities. So they
went out into the alley, and they caught both of the cats
in their little pranks. So they sent them to the Humane
Society, and the Humane Society sent them back because
they did not want them. And that's what they did. You
see, the year right now is 2020. And they took them to a
cat place, you know, where cats eat with spoons, and
they have meetings, and they play around. So, they
kinda adopted the place after a while, and it just gets
kinda neat.

*Moral: I guess you could probably say the moral is like killing
two birds with one stone, 'cause they went out and caught both
of the cats. They didn't kill them, but they got them.*

## ANALYSIS

This story proved to be an exceedingly rich one. The
two cats are the child's personal representatives, his
"good" and "bad" parts. There is evidence here of a
prominent use of splitting, as well as of concretization.
The selection of "cats" as a personal representative
seemed at once to reflect Sean's impulsive nature, his
pseudoautonomy, and his aggressiveness, which had
an oral-sadistic core. The "scratchy" cat at times seems
to act in concert with the "playful" cat, although at
other times it is held solely responsible for the mischief
it creates. We are not surprised to learn that the
"scratchy" cat's impulsivity has rather predictably
alienated its owners, who finally reject both of the cats.
These cats, however, are so undesirable and incorrigi-
ble that not even the Humane Society will take them
in. In the story's conclusion, there is an attempt at once
both magical and desperate to transform multiple ex-

periences of rejection into the assertive adoption of a new home, with a fairly transparent allusion to the group home environment.

Sean's narrative account was especially valuable in that it provided significant psychodiagnostic information about his nuclear conflict and characteristic defensive operations at a very early point in the treatment process. Sean's expectation, like that of many children whose early histories are fraught with traumatic separations and whose attachments are consequently ambivalent, is that his basic needs for emotional support and stability will remain unmet, not unlike those of the two cats. Moreover, once others come to know him, they will recognize him for what he is, and history will repeat itself, with yet another painful rejection. A number of his subsequent stories (one of them reproduced in Chapter 4) both confirmed the nuclear significance of this abandonment/rejection motif and supplied regular opportunities to assess clinical improvement. Gradually, Sean developed a better understanding of his mother's psychological limitations and her motives for placing him in foster care. He was able for perhaps the first time to understand and express genuine sorrow over this loss and to place his own contributions in a more reality-based (and forgiving) perspective.

## THE CASE OF ROBERT

Robert was a ten-year-old whose academic performance had declined steadily despite his high intelligence and the ambitious efforts of both his teachers and his parents. There was also a history of provocative and hostile behavior toward his three siblings and, to a lesser extent, his parents. He frequently violated minor rules at home, was stubborn and noncompliant, and had recently resorted to throwing temper tantrums when he was unable to get his own way. Perhaps on good behavior for my benefit, Robert required little prompting to tell the following story during his initial diagnostic interview:

---

### ROBERT'S STORY

Once upon a time, a long time ago, there was a Prince that was planning on marrying a Princess of a King that lived about a mile away. And the Prince invited the Princess and he had a Grand Ball. They had their wedding session and they didn't know it, but these wicked creatures got invited along with all the other guests. One of the creatures really wanted the Prince and Princess to be bad. This creature appeared in the form of a goose with wings on it, and she said, "The next baby you have will die of thirst and nothing will help it." And so, they had a baby. And a couple of weeks later, it started getting skinnier and skinnier, and you could see its bones popping out. And the Prince and Princess, they took him to the Royal Treatment Center, and the Treatment Center couldn't do anything, so they just let it die. The baby was blind, but it wasn't wicked. *Moral: You shouldn't always have to be mean or wicked. You can be nice sometimes and sometimes you can be mean.*

### ANALYSIS

A sad and tragic tone seemed to pervade Robert's story, in which he revealed some vitally important information about himself and his view of the world. The Prince and Princess can be seen as parent-representatives, and the tragically flawed infant as Robert himself, who was undersized for his age and had to wear corrective lenses because of poor vision. In his story, Robert depicts himself as a victim of circumstances, a small and completely vulnerable infant whose inability to derive sustenance and oral gratifications from his environment is the result of an evil spell cast over his parents; he suggests that the Prince and Princess are not responsible for the tragic fate that befalls their infant son, although they do appear to disregard the warning of the wicked goose. This is a child for whom there is no hope, only the inevitability of (psychological) starvation and death.

Robert's mother was a woman in her late thirties who related cordially, if obsessionally, during the interview. Her focus on her son's behavior showed little recognition of her role in contributing to his emotional reactions, although he often became petulant and oppositional in direct consequence of her inability to allow him psychological distance. What she saw as an appropriate level of maternal concern and involvement not only was excessive but also powerfully communicated both her guilt and the expectation that her son really could not function well enough on his own—an expectation, according to the history the parents were able to provide, that was established before Robert turned two. His father was a warm, emotionally accessible individual who was able to relate to Robert in a more natural, empathic, and less conflicted way, although his influence was largely eclipsed by that of Robert's mother.

Returning to Robert's story, it now seems possible to understand the "wicked creatures," and especially the goose, as negative maternal introjects. Robert's rage has a narcissistic core and is directed at his mother both because he holds her responsible for his small size and poor vision and because his mother by her actions has confirmed his greatest fear—that without her he will not be able to survive. His mother's historical inability to respond empathically to his needs has left him with an unstable and unconsolidated self-identity. The fact that the infant's fate is incontrovertible despite the heroic measures performed at the "Royal Treatment Center" (i.e., the mental health agency) is a profound expression of this child's despair.

The moral, which does not at first appear to have direct bearing upon the story, actually contains a statement with a great deal of psychological meaning. In his admonishment that people should be "mean" some of the time and "nice" at other times, Robert is really describing his mother's difficulty in modulating her own affective involvement with him. His subjective experience of her is of a rigid person whose "meanness" (empathic failure) has had far-reaching ramifications for his psychological growth.

Although its full clinical significance could not be grasped immediately, Robert's story provided a point of departure for hypothesis making and later therapeutic investigation. On a purely intuitive level, it served to establish the fragility of Robert's self-esteem and the degree to which his narcissistic integrity had been compromised by repeated injury. Notably, this thematic material was not nearly as distinctly represented in Robert's other productions and activities during the diagnostic phase as in this initial autogenic story.

## THE CASE OF DAVID

David, an attractive, bright-eyed nine-year-old boy, was referred because of escalating physical aggressiveness with peers, poor school performance, pathological lying, and generalized anxiety. David's parents had been divorced less than a year before his mother, acceding to a recommendation made by David's pediatrician, brought him in for treatment; his problems had greatly intensified shortly after custody was awarded to her. David's father was a seriously disturbed individual subject to periods of psychotic depression. Shortly before his parents were divorced, David walked into the garage at the fortuitous moment to discover his father, barely alive, hanging by a necktie from one of the support beams. David's swift response to his father's attempted suicide was credited with saving his life. The psychological sequelae, however, were awesome. Most of David's symptoms, including recurrent nightmares in which this terrifying event was relived over and over again, dated back to the circumstances surrounding the father's psychotic break and subsequent hospitalization. David told the following story during the first diagnostic interview:

---

### DAVID'S STORY ("HOW FROGS GOT BULGY EYES")

Once upon a time, there was a frog on the sidewalk. There was also a big cat, and the cat saw the frog and started running after him. The little frog managed to escape, but he was taking real big breaths. He wasn't re-

ally looking out, and someone came along and stepped
on top of him. Then his eyes got all bulgy.
*Moral: It's a dangerous world.*

## ANALYSIS

Though told without much drama, this is a very disturbing and highly personal narrative. It is the story
of a child who has come to experience life as a recurrent bad dream, and whose self-experience is that of a
passive actor who barely has enough time to draw a
deep breath between the blows. Yet the frog in
David's story is not nearly as vulnerable a self-repre-
sentation as the infant in Robert's story, nor as helpless to act. David's frog has sustained a series of
painful traumata, but he has thus far managed to survive. David's own strength and partial success in coping with his difficult family situation was probably
due in large measure to the essentially positive relationship he had with his mother. Mrs. B. was a sensitive and generous individual who derived a great deal
of satisfaction from raising David and his older sister.
Indeed, she was generally quite successful in match-
ing her affection and maternal attention to her children's psychological needs.

Although the "world is a dangerous place" according to David's moral, the greatest dangers appear to
lie within. David's repressed guilt and his maladaptive expression of anger made the world feel much
more dangerous as he projected his most disturbing
wishes and greatest fears outward. That guilt and the
rage that David experienced over his father's suicide
attempt and his parent's divorce, along with the am-

bivalent relationship that had evolved between David and his father, became important foci of his treatment.

Autogenic stories, like dreams, are subject to the principle of multiple determination. It is the rare story that seems to permit only a single interpretation or explanation. The assumption of such clinical ambiguity is a particularly important principle of diagnostic assessment, in which the focus is on generating clinical hypotheses. In effect, it is the ongoing process of treatment that establishes an evidentiary base that either supports or fails to confirm early clinical hypotheses, or leads the clinician to modify them. For instance, one can alternatively understand both the cat and the person who inadvertently steps on the frog as David's personal representatives. The frog could be seen as a father-representative toward whom David feels considerable anger, guilt, and disappointment. The frog's "bulging eyes" and breathlessness then come to represent the ghastly image of David's father hanging in the garage, gasping for air. Whether this interpretation of David's story ultimately possesses the same degree of accuracy as the first interpretation is perhaps less important than its value in alerting the clinician to a somewhat different, though related dynamic issue—the storyteller's anger and guilt over having been unfairly thrust into an adult role. Subsequent stories and other clinical data will furnish a more satisfactory answer.

## The Case of Carl

Carl was eleven years old when he was referred by his school psychologist to a family service agency for diagnostic assessment. A petulant, provocative boy whose waif-like appearance

made him look a bit like the poster child for Boy's Town, Carl
was severely troubled and borderline. His disturbing range of
symptoms included secondary encopresis (a regressive return
to fecal soiling following successful toilet training), antisocial
behavior, multiple facial tics, aggressive behavior toward his
siblings and peers, school refusal, and suicidal threats and gestures.

Relationships between Carl and both of his parents were exceedingly poor, with Carl's provocative behavioral style often
engendering punitive and sometimes abusive responses from
his mother and his father. Carl was nearly incapable of tolerat-
ing even minor frustrations and had very little control over his
aggressive impulses. Psychological testing failed to reveal any
specific learning disabilities, although IQ testing placed him between dull normal and minimally retarded. Carl alternately told
his parents how much he hated them and threatened to kill himself in order to get even with them. On at least one occasion he
was treated and released from a community hospital following a
minor self-inflicted knife wound.

After some prodding in the first diagnostic interview, Carl
told this story:

_____

CARL'S STORY

Once upon a time, No. 47's house caught on fire. Her
kitchen and living room roof collapsed. All the people
managed to get out of the house before it burned
down. My neighbor, Sue, burnt to a crisp, though.
Everyone was sad to see the house go, but there was a
good part of it, because the house was rebuilt one
month later.

*Moral: Never play with matches or with a stove.*

ANALYSIS

Carl's story was especially helpful not because it provided new or revealing information but because it confirmed already-forming clinical intuitions. The story dramatically illustrates not only the magnitude of this child's hostile-aggressive wishes but also the paucity of conflict-free solutions available to his ego. Hyperaggressive children frequently make use of the mechanism of undoing ("the house was rebuilt one month later") to defend against their destructive wishes. The story also exposes the degree to which Carl's ego integrity is compromised by the expression of his rage: Carl's remark about his neighbor Sue "burning up" reveals a blurring of primary and secondary process contents. (Just a few days earlier, Sue had reprimanded him for beating up a smaller neighborhood child.) Although Carl had been asked to compose a story that had make-believe characters as well as make-believe content, his use of the possessive pronoun and his neighbor's real name suggests that for him fantasy and reality are continuous for him, rather than two distinct modes of experience.

The structural deficiency of Carl's superego is apparent in the moral to his story. The moral, which makes the story sound like a cautionary tale, reflects neither self-awareness nor a truly internalized sense of right and wrong. It speaks to the story in much the same way that a parent speaks to a three-year-old child: "Don't play with matches because you can hurt yourself." The moral has a false ring to it and is no more than a gratuitous offering to the clinician in the interest of making the story somewhat more socially acceptable.

Although intensive psychotherapy (plus adjunctive family counseling) was recommended for Carl, his parents were not convinced of its value and withdrew him from treatment after several months. When I saw him again some eighteen months later at their urgent request, Carl had decompensated dramatically. In addition to his continuing difficulties with aggression and increasingly serious suicidal gestures, he had developed a dangerous sexual obsession with his mother. Outpatient treatment was unfortunately no longer a viable alternative, and Carl had to be hospitalized in a long-term adolescent inpatient program.

## USING SQUIGGLE DRAWINGS IN CONJUNCTION WITH DIAGNOSTIC STORIES

Because autogenic stories are projective and involve a natural method of narration requiring only basic verbal skills that most children have already mastered, they are often useful as a vehicle for surmounting initial resistance. For certain children, however, the direct expression of unconscious fantasies and fears may provoke severe anxiety reactions even when disguised through the medium of a projective story. It is nevertheless possible to elicit stories from such children if the storytelling is not completely autogenous in nature. Imaginative stories composed in conjunction with drawings prove useful not only as sources of valuable dynamic information but also, in the early phase of treatment, as bridges from which the therapist can forge an affective tie and begin a meaningful therapeutic discourse. Playing the *squiggle* drawing-completion game produced rich diagnostic data in projective form in both of the cases vignetted that follow.

## THE CASE OF DANNY

Six-year-old Danny was referred for evaluation and treatment following a report of physical abuse by his father. Although there was a long history of violent marital arguments and of psychological abuse of both Danny and his younger sister, neither child had ever been seen for assessment or treatment. When his father pushed him down against the bathtub, Danny sustained several facial cuts and a black eye; at the time of his first interview, he still had residual discoloration and scars from the facial lacerations. Slow to warm up, he initially participated only in a somewhat suspicious, tentative way. He refused to tell a story and didn't seem particularly interested in other play modalities, either. It took a second frustrating session before Danny showed any interest in the squiggle game, and even then, his enthusiasm was less than optimal.

Danny turned my opening squiggle into a snail and then told me this story:

---

### DANNY'S STORY

Once upon a time, there was a snail running through the grass. Then he stopped at a hole. He looked inside

of it and saw nothing but black dark. Then, "BOO!" He
fell into the hole. Then a little kitten came and got him
out, and ate him.

## ANALYSIS

This story, which contains several vitally important elements, proved to be a very important early communication for Danny. It is told with a depressed and
hopeless tone, and describes the self-experience of a
child who has come to regard the world as a place
filled with dangers and malevolent forces that threaten
both his psychological and his physical integrity. The
choice of the snail as a personal representative, in my
own experience not an unusual one for children who
have been traumatized, speaks to both his smallness
and fragility and a prominent defensive mode: psychic
withdrawal.

Although Danny remained resistant to producing a
true autogenic story, we did come up with a number of
subsequent squiggle-stories together. He gradually became significantly less anxious and depressed, and
made good clinical progress despite persistent uncer-
tainties and environmental deficits in his family life.
While he was in treatment, his parents separated more
or less permanently, and his mother was awarded full
physical custody of both Danny and his younger sister.
Danny's father was adjudicated and placed on proba-
tionary status, so that Danny no longer had any contact with him. When, later, his mother was preparing
to move from the area with both children, she reported

that Danny, despite occasional setbacks, continued to make a good adjustment.

## The Case of Annie

Four-and-a-half-year-old Annie had caused some concern at her day-care center when staff observed her purposely injuring herself, for no apparent reason. She was also obsessively preoccupied with morbid themes and talked about them with other children and staff members. Her mother reported that Annie's maternal grandfather had died shortly before these clinical signs appeared, attributing Annie's symptoms to her depression over the loss. Actually, Annie was more concerned with the psychological unavailability of her mother, who was still in mourning; additionally, she was displaying signs of reactive depression in response to her mother's intensified romantic involvement with a boyfriend of several months. Annie's mother and father had separated before Annie was born, and until she met her current boyfriend, her mother had not permitted herself to become "seriously involved" with a man. She had always maintained that the responsibilities of managing her life and Annie's, combined with her full-time professional career, made such a relationship too difficult, perhaps even "burdensome."

After a few unsuccessful attempts to elicit an autogenic story from Annie, I began to play the squiggle game with her. She clearly enjoyed this reciprocal endeavor and soon produced and completed a squiggle drawing showing a little doll and a large man. She then spontaneously told a story that revealed completely unexpected information: On at least two occasions, a thirteen-year-old male cousin had forced Annie into a bathroom where he exposed himself to her and asked her to touch his penis; terrified, she had refused. Nevertheless, Annie had to continue to see the cousin during family visits because her mother did not take the incidents very seriously.

Annie's story explained her distress and clarified the corresponding clinical features.

---

## ANNIE'S STORY

He made himself naked and the little dolly is laughing at him. He is very big. The dolly is afraid of him. He holds onto his thing in front and goes to the bathroom. When he asks the girl to hold onto it (she's only two), she doesn't like that.

## ANALYSIS

Because I believed that Annie had more or less accurately represented a frightening experience involving sexual victimization, I departed from my usual procedure of working within the metaphor and asked her directly about the personal significance of her drawing and story. (I also informed her mother and then made a report to child protective services.)

The depiction of the self as a doll speaks poignantly to the powerlessness and vulnerability Annie had experienced in the course of the traumatic incidents with her cousin. Annie's symptoms remitted within several weeks of the session, and she has remained symptom-free. Although that was certainly in part a result of her mother's enhanced sensitivity to Annie's abandonment fears and the completion of her own grief-work, it was due equally to Annie's emotional expression of the trauma and the therapeutic response to it.

It is, of course, a matter of therapeutic discretion whether one approaches such story-metaphors in a direct interpretive way. Since children don't react well to such a breach of the "rules," one should have a strong rationale for making this kind of intervention. Indeed, as suggested earlier, the intervention is defensible in cases where a child's physical safety may be endangered. Besides, it is always possible to revisit the situation with the child in a subsequent interview to explore the reasons for the therapist's actions and the child's reaction to them.

## THE CASE OF DEREK

Derek, a rotund and rather shy ten-year-old, was referred to a family service agency because of declining academic performance and mild behavioral difficulties at school and at home. He lived with his maternal aunt, who had assumed legal custody of Derek when his mother was hospitalized for inpatient treatment of her alcoholism. By agreement with the Department of Social Services and with Derek's approval, he had remained with his aunt and uncle after his mother's release into a halfway-house program a month later; he stayed there throughout most of the time he was in treatment. I found Derek to be quite cooperative during our early encounters, but even after a couple of diagnostic interviews I still hadn't the sense that I really *knew* him, that I understood the nature of his behavioral problems or difficulties at school. He had attempted to compose an autogenic story at my request, but he steadfastly maintained that nothing came to mind. His frustration seemed quite genuine, so I suggested that instead we draw pictures together. Derek immediately agreed to this, at which point we started on squiggles. After each of us had taken a few turns, I asked Derek to compose a story based upon his completed drawing. He did so almost effortlessly, and with no further coaxing from me.

---

## DEREK'S STORY ("THE RIVER")

This is a river that is crazy and never stops emptying, and it has animals in it that never die. It also has food in it that never goes bad. And the most important thing is that the animals never go down the stream. Also, it's super because it's nice, fresh water, and half the cause of the animals never dying. The best and worst thing about "The River" is that if any person gets in it and gets outside it soon enough, then that person will never die. The worst part about it is that if you stay in it long enough, you'll die as soon as you get out of it.

## ANALYSIS

Derek's story contained a wellspring of dynamic information and yielded a far more intimate and detailed portrait of this disturbed youngster than I had been able to obtain up to that point. "The River" seemed to be Derek's way of symbolizing his relationship with his mother, a deeply troubling one that had posed nearly insurmountable obstacles for him. In the first place, Derek's river is "crazy," an allusion to her disturbing alcoholic behavior. Of additional significance is the intrauterine imagery here. The river appears to offer protection to the animals that live in it, but there is a catch: They mustn't go downstream (Derek's way of representing psychological birth and individuation). Furthermore, immortality (or perhaps enduring psychological well-being) is ensured for those who venture out of the river as long as they have not remained in the water for too long—but if, on the other hand, one remains immersed for an extended period, physical/psychological separation from the river means certain and swift death.

Such a dilemma suggests the psychological struggle associated with separation-individuation, particularly the crisis of the rapprochement subphase (Mahler et al., 1975). This hypothesis gathered additional support as I gradually pieced together Derek's early development and his infantile relationship with his mother. Derek had been conceived during a very brief relationship that had ended prior to his birth. He had no contact with his birth father and was unable to learn very much about him from his mother. She in turn, because of her alcoholism, had been largely incapable of providing for any but the most basic of his physical needs. In consequence, she was often in dyssynchrony with him. The quality and intensity of her connection to Derek was also rather unpredictable; at times she viewed him as perhaps the sole source of meaning in her life, whereas at other times she experienced him as a great psychological burden.

Since there can be no object constancy when maternal supplies are both unpredictable and poorly matched to a child's developmental needs, it is not surprising that Derek found successful negotiation of the rapprochement crisis virtually impossible. Derek's story strongly suggests that it was the poor judgment or some other fatal flaw of the *creatures* in the river that led to their demise, rather than the *river's* misattunement or neglect in failing to assist its inhabitants in determining which "supplies" they required and for how long. The river could not confer strength or immunity because it possesses neither; the locus of responsibility in Derek's story is with the creatures, all of which probably stand for Derek.

Coming as it did in an early interview, this story offered important insights about Derek and the psychological traumata to which he had been chronically exposed from infancy onward—insights emerging initially in the form of clinical hypotheses and developing gradually as his therapy evolved. "The River" proved an especially generative narrative account and remained an important referent over the course of treatment.

## STORIES USED FOR EVALUATIVE PURPOSES

Both impressionistic evidence and quantitative research data appear to support the idea that children's autogenic stories may also be useful in evaluating a child's progress in psychotherapy. This is actually not a new idea, having been advanced as early as the mid-1930s by J. L. Despert and H. W. Potter in their pioneering study of children's stories. One might naturally expect that stories told later in the treatment process would include increasingly adaptive resolutions to conflict and demonstrate an overall maturation of ego functions. Indeed, compelling data support the notion that the child becomes increasingly able to incorporate into stories told later in treatment earlier resolutions and adaptations proposed by the therapist *per metaphor* (see Chapter 7). Moreover, that development can generally be correlated with parallel developments in the child's life outside of treatment.

## SUMMARY

Although stories and storytelling have a time-honored position in both diagnostic and therapeutic work with children, autogenic stories have generally not been used as a diagnostic or evaluative tool by the child clinician. When used for such purposes, however, they can provide the clinician with valuable data about the child's intrapsychic structure, characteristic conflicts, and repertoire of defensive adaptations. The initial diagnostic story can also serve as a kind of "life narrative," throwing into bold relief the child's most profound fears and conflicts. Because these issues are often not as clearly represented in other sources of clinical data, the autogenic story may serve a unique function in the diagnostic process. Even when the child's story does not contain such information, it can frequently provide the clinician with valuable projective data that may generate or perhaps confirm clinical hypotheses. Storytelling may also be usefully combined with unstructured drawing in work with children who might otherwise be disinclined to produce autogenic narratives, or who simply express a preference for such a pairing.

# CHAPTER 3

# Narrative and Historical Meaning in Child Psychotherapy

The psychodynamic literature on child diagnosis and assessment has traditionally emphasized the importance of data collection and integration as a prelude to treatment. As noted earlier, the therapist's observation of the child in both clinical and naturalistic settings and of the child's parents and siblings, the developmental history, psychological test reports, and consultations with teachers and pediatricians form a significant portion of the database. More detailed information regarding development of the ego and the self, development of libidinal and aggressive drives, and the child's use of defenses also contributes critically to the foundation from which meaningful treatment evolves.

The assumption that some pathogenic event has ultimately given rise to the child's specific symptoms and complaints has governed the assessment process as conceived historically and as still practiced. That assumption calls our attention to chronology and sequence, to the importance of working within a historical context to understand the development of psychopathology. Psychoanalysis has recognized for over a century the significance of the historical events and other phenomena that shape the personality, and has recognized, too, that the intricate fabric into which they are woven must finally be unraveled in order to explain the pathogenesis of emotional disturbance.

This interest has generated constructs such as the "complementary series," a scheme that seeks to determine the relative strength of constitutional and experiential factors in pathogenesis, and has also led to the *metapsychological perspective* generally referred to as the genetic point of view. The genetic viewpoint requires that the clinician and patient arrive at an understanding of the present through the laborious process of reconstructing the past, because we assume that the historical past persists into the present and that the human organism must be understood in a historical context. Freud's early position on the psychogenesis of hysteria in female patients, the seduction theory, is probably responsible for the original emphasis on genetic or historical antecedents of neurotic disturbance. In the original theory of the etiology of hysteria (Freud and Breuer, 1895), causality was attributed to patients' reports of sexual traumata, and these reports were presumed to be veridical recollections. But what Freud originally attributed to actual experiences of sexual traumata he later came to understand as evidence of neurotic wishes and conflicts that had persisted into

adulthood without having been satisfactorily re-
solved. Although this paradigmatic shift was critically
important in the evolution of psychoanalytic thought,
the focus on historical events was nevertheless re-
tained. Psychoanalytic interest remained centered on
historically significant internal events and the developmental significance of neurotic conflict.

## HISTORICAL AND NARRATIVE DISCOURSE: THEORETICAL PERSPECTIVES

Donald Spence (1982), for one, critically examined the
distinctions between narrative truth and historical
truth insofar as both exist in relation to the clinical enterprise of psychoanalysis. He defined narrative truth
as

> [t]he criterion we use to decide when a certain experience has
> been captured to our satisfaction; it depends on continuity and
> closure and the extent to which the fit of the pieces takes on an
> aesthetic finality. Narrative truth is what we have in mind when
> we say that such and such is a good story, that a given explana-
> tion carries conviction, that one solution to a mystery must be
> true. Once a given construction has acquired narrative truth, it
> becomes just as real as any other kind of truth; this new reality
> becomes a significant part of the psychoanalytic cure. (p. 31)

Spence argued that narrative truth is often mistaken
for historical truth, pointing out that a variety of factors make the likelihood of this error a strong one. For
example, he observed that Freud's dictum that the analyst should listen with evenly hovering attention can
never really be strictly adhered to in the clinical situa-

tion, inasmuch as the analyst must also listen "with an ear tuned to sequence, coherence, and transformation" (p. 22). In this sense, the analyst is judged by Spence to be listening actively, and interpolating his or her own constructs, associations, and secondary elaborations into the patient's account. It becomes a joint creation, a jointly authored narrative that may or may not accurately reflect the historical truths that are, Spence asserted, the true object of psychoanalytic inquiry. In developing his argument further, Spence declared that some of the most basic assumptions about what is communicated in the analytic situation, and whether these communications ever occur within a matrix of shared meanings, need to be questioned. For Spence, these and other issues form a serious threat to the scientific credibility of psychoanalytic theory and treatment.

Others have questioned whether, in fact, it is possible to uncover historical truths from psychoanalytic data in the first place. R. Schafer proposed that "there are no objective, autonomous, or pure psychoanalytic data which, as Freud was fond of saying, compel one" (1980, p. 30) to draw certain conclusions. Specifically, "there is no single, necessary, definitive account of a life history and psychopathology," according to Schafer. Furthermore, "what have been presented as the plain empirical data and techniques of psychoanalysis are inseparable from the investigator's precritical and interrelated assumptions concerning the origins, coherence, totality, and intelligibility of personal action" (1980, p. 30). Essentially, Schafer contended that it would be next to impossible to consider psychoanalytic data *except* in narrational terms, despite the assiduous efforts of classical psychoanalysis to ally itself with positivistic science. Schafer described psychoanalytic case histories and treatment histories in similar relativistic language: They are "tellings of human events," he said, "not measurements or simple records of process and materials in the physical universe" (1997, p. 92). He also observed that the psychoanalytic narrative is not based on a unitary model: Klein, Sullivan, Fairbairn, and Kohut all require narrative structures that are different from classical psychoanalysis and from each other. The process of telling and retelling stories—the patient's narrative accounts and the analyst's reworking of them through the vehicle of interpretation—results in an "interweaving of texts" and multiple transformations of the narrative; this process, Schafer maintained, is fundamental to the psychoanalytic endeavor. His fundamentally hermeneutic perspective, based on different ways of constructing meaning and of understanding human experience, has offered a radically different vision of not only of the clinical process but also the way in which the mind itself is conceived (Mitchell and Black, 1995).

S. Viderman (1979) asserted that the archaic and yet historically significant experiences of the patient cannot actually be rediscovered or reconstructed (to use Freud's archaeological metaphor) because they exist in a shadowy and fragmentary form. It is only through interpretive speech that such experiences become coherent and accessible to the psychoanalytic discourse. Viderman, too, seemed to suggest that historical truth is elusive and perhaps illusory as well. Interpretation is conceived not as a component in an analytic strategy to recover repressed historical truths (which may not be recoverable) but, rather, as a technique to open up new possibilities, introduce new evidence, and otherwise rework themes in a creative manner within the psychoanalytic dialogue.

The foregoing addresses the status of narrative and historical truths within the framework of adult psychoanalytic treatment, which is actually twice removed from the true focus of this chapter—the status of narrative and historical accounts within the frame of psychoanalytic psychotherapy with children. The child assessment process, to which we now return, often differs significantly from the assessment of adults—a distinction with multiple ramifications for this discussion.

### Clinical Assessment in Child Psychotherapy: The Cultivation and Synthesis of "Data"

The clinical assessment process in dynamic child psychotherapy is geared toward the collection and synthesis of both subjective and objective data, although the historical truths often become the more important source for both generating and validating clinical hypotheses. In this sense, the search for historical truths is a goal of the assessment phase; the product will become a referent throughout treatment.

The child psychotherapist is trained to place considerable emphasis on clinical inquiry within the framework of historical-developmental exploration and analysis. The search for historical meaning is initiated the moment the child's life is discussed in developmental terms with his or her parents, and it cannot fail to have an impact on the clinician's view of that child; sometimes, this is true even when clinical interviews with the child do not seem fully compatible with the historical data. (Although clinical experience has taught us that parents can be very poor historians, we often make the assumption that children are even worse historians, if only by virtue of their not having the integrative capacity for the recall of information prior to age five or six.) Indeed, there has been a proliferation of elaborate instruments for gathering salient developmental and other historical information, ever-more detailed symptom and behavior checklists, and, in general, an increasing reliance on quantitative data to guide us in approaching the child treatment enterprise more efficiently—all with the ultimate objective of establishing continuities between the present and the historical past. Whereas the child's history and the quest for historical meaning have been prominent foci of the diagnostic process, the clinician must now make a critical shift in order to engage in a distinctively different phenomenological task. In short, the clinician must initiate a narrative discourse with the child as a means of enhancing the unwinding of the child's life story. This narrative account reflects the child's experience of the historical truth imbued with highly personal meanings.

## The Narrative Discourse in Child Psychotherapy

The narrative discourse that commences with psychotherapy *proper* makes possible the evolution of a child's unique and personal story. There are several aspects of this narrative discourse that clearly distinguish it from the historical-developmental inquiry that characterizes the assessment process. In the first place, the emphasis on time and sequence and on the developmental paradigm that informs anamnesis or history taking must assume a secondary role because successful child treatment occurs in an *ahistorical* context. Time gives way to time*less*ness, so the rational, chronological ordering of events characteristic of the assessment process is of little utility. There is a continuous interweaving of themes and fantasies, and of conflict and defense, with no particular attention to the logic of sequence. Another difference between child assessment and child treatment that further underscores the need for a phenomenological accommodation has to do both with children's communicative processes and with the unique content of those communications. Developmental psychology has convincingly demonstrated that very young children, being largely incapable of inductive or deductive reasoning (Piaget, 1969), are far more likely to explain phenomena both to themselves and to others in a transductive fashion (i.e., from particular to particular). An important corollary of this, of course, is children's relatively greater reliance on the primary process mode. Although it is not difficult to obtain primary process material from adults via dream analysis and free association, this "language" (i.e., the primary process made of communication) has already become unfamiliar, superseded by secondary process thought and reasoning. With children, particularly younger children, access to the primary process mode is relatively uncomplicated: Its content is generated quite readily in their spontaneous play, verbalized fantasies and stories, and productions.

A more complicated task, and one that is far more difficult for the therapist in making the critical transition from assessment to treatment, is creating and maintaining the necessary therapeutic environment to enhance and cultivate the unfolding of the child's narrative account. And it is not enough simply to allow the child to express primitive fantasies, regressive wishes, fears, or conflicts; the therapist must extract the child's narrative from these fragmentary communications. Furthermore, every effort must be made to understand this emerging narrative as *the child's own and unique version* of the histories that have been the focus of the assessment process. The failure to consider the child's story from the earliest points of contact can only restrict both the flow and the content of this narrative discourse, leading almost inevitably to unfavorable therapeutic results.

Indeed, it is likely that a failure of empathic rapport between clinician and child begins, in essence, as soon as the clinician attempts to superimpose historical "truths" on the child's narrative accounts in order to gauge their "accuracy." Although such a framework appears to lend coherence and continuity to the therapeutic task, it may also alienate child from clinician and lead to a therapeutic misalliance. The child therapist must accept the child's evolving narrative as a verisimilitude even when it does not correspond to the historical facts, a perspective that in the literary and fine arts would be termed *the willing suspension of disbelief*.

## AUTOGENIC STORIES: ROYAL ROAD TO THE CHILD'S NARRATIVE

A number of techniques in dynamic child psychotherapy have served as effective vehicles for the unwinding of the child's narrative. Through a variety of representational play activities, the therapist seeks to create a climate of trust and to establish a meaningful affective tie with the child. The choice of play techniques is multifactorial: Different toys, play media, and activities appeal to children of different developmental ages, and children soon reveal their own strong interests or preferences. And, of course, both the strengths and the limitations in the therapist's repertoire of technical skills will influence the nature and variety of therapeutic play.

But autogenic stories in particular, either those that are completely stimulus-free or those told in conjunction with unstructured drawing games, have proven especially effective in eliciting the child's narrative—for two basic reasons. First, listening to and telling stories is a familiar, experience-near mode of communication for young children and one that affords pleasure to the vast majority of children under the age of thirteen. Second, the child's metaphorical story communications are relatively free of the therapist's influence, a requirement that is not always easy to meet in the therapeutic playroom. There is now an extensive literature on the various ways in which children's stories can be used with or without artistic productions, sociodramatic play, and therapeutic games, and as either a technique or a method in dynamic child psychotherapy.

The following clinical vignette demonstrates the distinguishing attributes of the autogenic story as a medium for communicating the child's narrative. It also establishes the importance of the child's narrative as a unique retelling of the historical account. Further, it points to the critical importance of the therapist's empathic resonance with the child's unique version of the case history. Finally, it illustrates the power of the therapist's participation in this narrational process when the autogenic story is used not only as a vehicle for the child's narrative but also as a medium for therapeutic communications *per metaphor*.

## THE CASE OF JED

Jed, a ten-year-old boy referred by another psychotherapist for individual treatment, lived with his mother, stepfather, five-year-old brother, and eighteen-month-old half-sister. He was an exceedingly bright, likable child with a vivid imagination and seemed an especially good candidate for psychoanalytically oriented individual treatment. Very small and seemingly quite fragile physically, Jed was being carefully monitored at a pediatric endocrinology clinic at the time treatment began; his location on a growth chart below the fifth percentile had aroused clinical suspicion that he suffered from psychosocial dwarfism. That possibility was later ruled out, but his short stature was one of a number of issues he presented in treatment.

Jed had a highly pathological relationship with his mother, Mrs. D., with whom he had lived for six of his ten years. Mrs. D. had historically experienced Jed as a poorly behaved and unlikable child. She was at times openly hostile toward him, though not consistently so, having demonstrated some capacity for containment of her hostile-aggressive feelings. Their relationship deteriorated dramatically following the birth of Jed's younger brother, whom Mrs. D. regarded as much more loving and manageable.

Jed had relatively little contact with his natural father, a convicted ex-felon residing in a distant part of the country, to mitigate the pain of his day-to-day life in this rejecting and hostile environment. Moreover, he had experienced a series of painful, traumatogenic losses: his uncle had recently been convicted of multiple counts of pederasty against a group of young boys; his baby sister (whose picture he still carried in his wallet) and a slightly older girl cousin had both succumbed to sudden infant death syndrome (SIDS) within the last few years; and, shortly after Jed began treatment with me, the fiancé of Mrs. D's younger sister, a young man with whom he was very close, was killed, in a contract-style execution, by Jed's maternal grandmother, who was subsequently convicted of first-degree murder.

The referring psychotherapist, a woman, had worked with Jed for over a year with some success. She felt, however, that he desperately needed to work with a male therapist, inasmuch as he had achieved resolution of neither the paternal abandonment issues nor the traumatogenic events surrounding his uncle's arrest and the death of his aunt's fiancé. The transition was not an easy one for Jed or his family, but he was able to discuss it soon after we began to work together.

Jed seemed especially intrigued with the unstructured drawing and reciprocal storytelling I suggested in an early diagnostic interview, and it later became a semiregular feature of his therapy sessions. This was Jed's first diagnostic story:

---

## JED'S STORY ("HENRY BEE")

Once Henry Bee saw a blue spruce tree and he flew and landed on it, and saw a pretty blue flower, and went down to get some pollen. Then he saw a blue house and went and flew into its window. There sat a blue lamp that he flew into, and then he got burnt and died. The End.

## ANALYSIS

Although this story is short, it is an impressive introduction to the rich narrative that later began to evolve in treatment. Henry Bee is, of course, Jed's personal representative. Henry is characterized as a lone figure whose efforts to extract pollen and derive warmth from a lamp are depicted as perilous ventures that eventually result in his death. There are few real gratifications in Henry's life, a life whose loneliness and false hopes seem to lead to this inevitable outcome. The lamp appears to serve as a metaphor for all the important relationships Henry has sought with members of his family: There is the promise of warmth and enlightenment, but real intimacy cannot be achieved because the price is far too great. The tone of the story and the obsessively repetitive use of the color "blue" convey the depression and hopelessness that both protagonist and storyteller must feel. Furthermore, a bee, being small and venomous, is in this sense a near-perfect choice for a boy whose physical and emotional vulnerabilities engender in him powerful and destructive hostile-aggressive feelings.

A week later, during our second diagnostic interview, Jed told this next story, also based on a squiggle-completion drawing:

---

Jᴇᴅ's Sᴛᴏʀʏ ("Tʜᴏᴍᴀs ᴛʜᴇ Wᴇᴀsᴇʟ")

Once upon a time, there was a weasel named Thomas, who went outside on a dark and dreary day. It started to pour, thunder, and lightning, and just when he was beginning to get scared, he saw an umbrella. Although he tried very hard to get to the umbrella, he was hit in the tail by lightning. He ran with his burnt tail, and jumped under the umbrella. The umbrella was struck by lightning and it killed him. The End.

Aɴᴀʟʏsɪs

If there was even the slightest reason for hope in the first story, there seems to be absolutely no possibility of it here. This is the story of a child who has come to view the world as a dangerous place filled with malevolent forces. To venture out and act autonomously carries with it the risk of annihilation. Jed also represents himself as a "weasel," an animal that must steal from others in order to survive, and that relies on its cunning to do so. Like a weasel, Jed had procured what few supplies were made available to him through stealth and deception, and always with a sense of imminent personal danger.

Jed seemed especially gratified that I was taking detailed notes as he told this story, at one point referring to me as his "secretary." By the time he told his next one, we had moved from the diagnostic evaluation to treatment proper, and I felt more confident about offering a therapeutic story-response. In the story reproduced here, which was told several months into treatment, Jed furnishes evidence of an important new theme.

---

### JED'S STORY ("THE LITTLE SQUEAK")

Once upon a time, there was a little "squeak" and he liked to go around in people's houses and go "squeak." He'd go "squeak" here and there . . . and then he'd go "squeak" all the way home. Right before he died, he went "squeak," and after he died, the other person went "squeak."

*Moral: If you squeak, you'll get squeaked back at.*

### ANALYSIS

Here, a small mouse-like creature appears to make a series of feeble attempts to engage in dialogue with those around him. Like Henry Bee and Thomas the Weasel, the Little Squeak is unsuccessful and ultimately dies unfulfilled. The moral seems to suggest that such efforts at communication are rewarded, although the story's sad ending leads to a rather different and much less hopeful conclusion. I understood Jed's story as a cautiously expressed wish to develop a more meaningful and gratifying discourse with the world around him and, I believed, with me in particular. Nevertheless, there is no acknowledgment of the Little Squeak's capacity for altering the inexorable and tragic scenario as it unfolds. Even the Little Squeak's death is but a whimper.

With this understanding of Jed's story, I told the following story in response:

---

### THERAPIST'S RESPONSE ("THE LITTLE SQUEAK")

Once upon a time, there was a Little Squeak who used to go around squeaking in a very high voice. He'd go "squeak" here and there, in peoples' houses, and lots of other places, too. Well, people became concerned about him after a while, and they called in some experts. The experts examined him. They couldn't find anything wrong with his heart or lungs, or with his bones, or with his blood or anything else. They were puzzled, and finally called in an expert on language. This expert listened carefully to the Little Squeak for a long time, and then recorded a few of his "squeaks" with a tape recorder. Then he slowed the tape down. When he played it back, the Little Squeak was actually saying, "Please pay attention to me. No one ever listens to me." The language expert then worked with him so that the Little Squeak could say things more slowly in order for other people to understand him better.

*Moral: When people hide their feelings, or express them in a way no one can understand, they usually go unnoticed. If you want people to notice you and listen to you, you have to speak slowly, and clearly, and directly, too.*

## Discussion

This therapeutic response attempts to acknowledge and address the Little Squeak's pain, Jed's disguised and unanswered cry for empathic recognition. It also reframes Jed's narrative by incorporating a therapy metaphor: The discourse in the responding version is a therapeutic discourse between the Little Squeak and the "language expert." Finally, it alters Jed's ending, in that the Little Squeak and the language expert now work together to enable the Little Squeak to communicate his psychological needs more successfully. The moral in the response-story arises naturally from the original but contains a reformulation of the therapeutic communication designed to appeal to the child's ego—to wit: When one makes an effort to be understood, recognition and empathic attention from others are far more likely to come. Jed seemed to enjoy the responding story a good deal and actually asked that I retell it. The idea that even a "Little Squeak" can be heard held great appeal for him and must have signified that he would have a standing opportunity in our sessions to be heard in whatever voice he cared to use.

Not long afterward, both Jed's mother and his classroom teacher contacted me, expressing alarm over two incidents in which Jed had been involved on a single day: He had attempted to hitch a ride on a garbage truck and had run in front of a moving train on a dare. Fortunately, he was not injured in either instance. In his next session, he evinced little awareness of either the tragic potential of such dangerous acting-out or what may have motivated this behavior. He did tell the following story, however.

---

### JED'S STORY ("PECOS BILL AND THE TREE")

Everyone's heard the story of Pecos Bill. Well, it's all a lie. I'm going to tell you the true story. . . . Once Pecos Bill was riding along the shore of the Gulf of Mexico. Pecos Bill was about to hit a tree. He looked at it and thought, "What a funny shape that tree has." He thought, but thought so hard that he ran right into it, into that tree. That was the end of Pecos Bill.

### ANALYSIS

In this story, Jed actually revealed one of the motives that appear to have contributed to his dangerous acting-out. Pecos Bill (his personal representative) is depicted as a loner, riding on a long journey along the Gulf Stream shore. Not only is Pecos Bill's judgment impaired (he runs into the tree after having seen it), but he also appears to be suffering from a sort of depersonalization reaction. The tree looks "funny" to him, and he finds this thought to be so preoccupying and anxiety-arousing that he rides into the tree and is killed by it. "Riding into the tree" may be explained as a way of combating an intolerable ego-state of nonfeeling and inner deadness; Pecos Bill rides into the tree to abort this unendurable deadness—that is, as a counterdissociative solution to the overwhelming anxiety often associated with the experience of depersonalization. Like his character Pecos Bill, Jed also suffers from a sense of inner depletedness and deadness, which at times he has found unbearably painful.

Armed with this understanding of his story, I felt able to explain Jed's dangerous acting-out as serving a similar counterdissociative function for him. (Not surprisingly, it later came to light that Jed's father had visited him shortly before the two incidents. Because the visit had been a very disturbing one for Jed, it seems likely that his principal means of defense against the massive anxiety it evoked was depersonalization, leading to his dangerous acting-out as a behavioral measure to counteract the ensuing inner deadness.) Hence, the following response-story from me.

---

THERAPIST'S RESPONSE
("THE TRUE-TO-LIFE STORY OF PECOS BILL")

Pecos Bill was a cattleman who frequently rode along the Gulf Stream shore. When he was alone, he sometimes felt very empty, and things looked strange or funny to him. When that happened, he would become frightened, and try to make himself feel better. Sometimes, he would even hurt himself and do dangerous things like running into trees just to feel less scared and sad. But he could also remind himself, when he felt lonely, that the feelings wouldn't last. . . . He would feel better. Sometimes, talking to his horse helped, and at other times, finding a companion to make the trip with him would also be helpful. Then he wouldn't feel the same need to get rid of the funny feelings and the scary thoughts that used to come with them. *Morals: When you are lonely and empty, ask for things.*

*Bad feelings don't last forever; they go away, and you can help make them go away by reaching out to people and animals when you feel bad.*

*There are less dangerous ways of getting rid of bad thoughts and feelings than by hurting yourself.*

### Discussion

The therapeutic message in my responding story was designed to accomplish several tasks: to help Jed acknowledge and examine the chronic emptiness and loneliness he himself feels through the Pecos Bill character, to convey to Jed my awareness of his urgent need to get rid of such intolerable thoughts and feelings, and to propose several safer alternatives to dangerous counterdissociative acts. The reminder that "Bad feelings don't last forever" was included in the responding story because it infuses a bit of hope into the story-dialogue. It may also serve more specifically as a bridge between the child's embattled and depleted self and my comparatively greater self-confidence and realistic optimism.

As the treatment relationship intensified, Jed began to tell a very different kind of story, one that seemed to reflect an entirely different dimension of the narrative account that had begun to evolve through his storytelling.

---

### JED'S STORY ("THE 'A' FROM AHSWA")

Once there was an "A" from the planet Ahswa. He looked very messy and everybody made fun of him because he wore earthling chapstick. The chapstick was cherry-flavored, and he was a squiggle that somebody made up. So he left Earth to find the person who created him. And nobody knows where he is. The End.

### ANALYSIS

Jed eloquently expresses the painful self-consciousness he experiences because of his diminutive stature. An even more important feature, however, is his communication of the protagonist's quest for self-identity and self-constancy. This story may be understood as an expression of Jed's confusion over who he is and whom he resembles, as well as how he came to be and, indeed, whether he exists with continuity through time and space. Jed has come to feel like a being from another planet, whose behavior is frequently strange and alienating to others. Although the "A" is capable of traversing the galaxy, he must protect his lips by wearing "earthling chapstick." He is a peculiar, fragile, alien creature who finally disappears with nary a trace.

My story-response attempts to address those issues, but also to reintroduce therapeutic communications from earlier story-dialogues with Jed. In this way, the narrative unfolding between child and therapist as their texts interweave becomes gradually consolidated into a story whose retelling becomes the essence of the treatment.

---

THERAPIST'S RESPONSE ("THE 'A' FROM AHSWA")

Once upon a time, there was an "A" from the planet Ahswa. This "A" felt very upset inside, and he was often neglected at home where people didn't have much time for him. He wanted very much to be like other kids, but felt different from them, and was very upset about this, too. Sometimes he felt almost as if he weren't there, like he could disappear and no one would ever notice. He wanted very much to find out who he was, and where he came from, and so he went to visit a historian, a person who helps people learn about history. The historian began to work with him so they could both learn more about him, but the work depended a great deal on how much "A" was willing to reveal about himself. Because of this, their work took a great deal of time.

*Moral: Learning who you are is not an easy task, but it can be done.*

## Discussion

The character of the historian, whose role is to assist individuals in arriving at a new understanding of their personal histories, is introduced in this responding story; he is intended to be a thinly disguised therapist-representative. The elements of neglect at home and Jed's painful self-consciousness about his small stature, both pivotal in the earlier narratives and secondary themes in his original "A" story, are reintroduced here.

It is the hopeful tone of this final narrative told in the pretermination phase of Jed's treatment that stands in such stark contrast with his earlier stories.

---

### JED'S STORY ("THE LITTLE OLD HOUSE")

Once there was a little old house, and it was on top of an icy mountain and was sliding down. The people inside of it were scared, but they managed to get to the ground safely. They went out and found an old shack with a burning fireplace. They opened the door, and there was nobody home, and they went in and sat down by the fireplace. As they sat down, an old man stepped in and saw them shivering and cold. The old man let them stay at the house until they could find a way to get back to the United States. The End.

### ANALYSIS

Here again is a story with a rich texture and multiple meanings, the hopeful tone being perhaps its most significant feature. The psychotherapy itself has brought the old house down from atop the icy mountain—a process that has clearly entailed dangerous risks to Jed, but one that seems to promise much more for his future than the icy isolation of his past and present. He also appears to have represented me as the "old man," and the therapy as a warm, nurturing way station en route to his final destination, the "United States." The "United States" may well be the integrated, consolidated self that Jed hopes to attain in treatment.

Although the clinician's skill in communicating empathic interest in the child's narrative account is always important, it is a sine qua non for work with severely traumatized children such as Jed. When handled with sensitivity, the clinician's therapeutic participation in the reworking of old narrative structures and the creation of new ones is not only tolerated but actually welcomed warmly, even by the most resistant child.

## SUMMARY

As illustrated by the extended examples of Jed's storytelling, the therapist's participation in the evolution of a child's narrative holds genuinely transformative power. In this chapter we explored the dialectical tension that exists between historical-developmental inquiry and narrative discourse in clinical work with children. We examined the distinctive role of the latter process, which characteristically emerges only after collective efforts have been made by the clinician and the child's parents to cultivate and synthesize historical data. We addressed the complex and sensitive nature of the clinician's task in developing and supporting the child's narrative discourse. And, finally, we identified the autogenic story as a useful vehicle for traversing the "royal road" to the child's narrative.

# CHAPTER 4

# Applications to Special Clinical Issues and Problems of Childhood

Clinical work with disturbed children and those felt to be otherwise at-risk has historically involved a wide range of play techniques and modalities—among them doll play, costume play, water play, puppetry, clay modeling, drawing, and the therapeutic use of games—although, at times, the traditional therapeutic play modalities simply cannot provide the child clinician either with sufficient, dynamically meaningful information about the child or with an effective vehicle for conveying both therapeutic understanding of the child's narrative and therapeutic communications of a more specific nature. All too often, those children most in need of the clinician's empathic understanding and interventive skills are also the children who pose the greatest challenge to the initiation and maintenance of a truly intersubjective discourse.

Accordingly, children's autogenic stories have long been recognized as an important source of clinical data. Such stories may reveal information about the child's intrapsychic structure, characteristic conflicts, defensive adaptations, and other aspects of ego functioning. They also may inform us about the nature and degree of the child's object relations and capacity for self and object constancy. They may provide us with information about disturbing wishes and fantasies or about the development and cohesiveness of the self and the coterminous attainment of higher forms of narcissism as well as other aspects of the child's character. Within a clinical framework of reciprocal storytelling and other play techniques, the resulting treatment process may lead to adaptive evolution of a child's narrative account, with such corresponding changes as increasingly adaptive alterations in defensive structure, in the ability to modulate affects and tolerate disappointments, in the taming of a harsh or overly punitive superego, or in the strengthening of self-structures.

Reciprocal storytelling appears to be a particularly versatile technique, seemingly as effective with more serious emerging disorders of character as with adjustment disorders or neurotic conflicts. The following examples illustrate the application of reciprocal storytelling to three very different clinical situations: a child negotiating an environmental crisis, a biracial girl with a selfobject disorder; and an eleven year-old boy with nascent borderline-like symptomatology.

## The Case of Sean—Revisited

### Responding to an Environmental Crisis

Sean, the eleven-year-old group home resident who told the story of the two cats (see Chapter 2), demonstrated an early interest in the storytelling procedure. Consequently, it became a regular feature of our twice-weekly sessions, a fortunate development for us both since he was not otherwise exactly enamored of our work. Actually, the storytelling process in this case both stabilized and enhanced a rather tenuous treatment relationship. The stories themselves served as bridges, supplying structure and continuity from one hour to the next. They also, however, gradually allowed me to enter Sean's inner world; and my own responding stories gave me the opportunity to convey my understanding to him.

Sean told the following story early in the middle phase of treatment. Although it centered on his characteristic abandonment/rejection motif, it was quite directly linked with, and triggered by, a specific environmental event. During the several preceding weeks, relations between the "treatment parents" and the rest of the staff at Sean's group home had deteriorated to the point where the couple no longer attended staff meetings or any other staff functions. They would generally even absent themselves from meals at the house as soon as the food was prepared.

Amidst considerable controversy over their inability and unwillingness to meet certain requirements that other staff members held to be essential in the treatment of the children in the home, the couple announced their decision to resign. No thought whatever was given to preparations for the customary farewell dinner in the face of such strong negative feelings, inasmuch as it would have more closely approximated a gesture of "good riddance." Therefore, it came as something of a surprise to discover that a small farewell party had been planned and executed by the children the evening prior to the couple's departure—the very evening Sean composed this story in therapy.

## SEAN'S STORY ("THE KING AND THE QUEEN")

Once upon a time, a long, long, long time ago . . . many
virtues [*sic*] of centuries ago . . . I mean just far, far back
. . . way, way, way, way back . . . actually, it's about a couple days ago [laughter] . . . there lived a [pause] small
king and his wife, the queen. They lived in England.
They were living happily happily ever after, meaning . . .
when they first became King and Queen, they were completely new to the . . . you could say, occupation, voca-
tion, job, or their specialty . . . or their dream. Well, these
people had seen a lot of harsh, weird things . . . happen
to (other) people. Other kings would get lots of people
after one person . . . or they'd get a dragon—you know,
"dragon spirits," as they say—after a person; incredibly,
that really happened. They became King and Queen and
they set the world at peace and they didn't make taxes or
anything. About four years after that, when the King re-
signed—he'd turned sixty-eight . . . he was sixty-five
when he . . . no, sixty-four when he first started and
turned sixty-eight and he decided it was time to quit. So
the people gave a big surprise party. The King and
Queen didn't know about this party. The whole country
came to the castle and they wished the King good luck
on his future. They made super giant cakes, two, four, six
of them about the size of a room. And everybody got a
piece. And everybody got some wine or milk, cherry
juice, or whatever they wanted [pause].

Well, the King and Queen were really surprised and
from that day on, they really didn't brag about being
the fairest or anything else. So, from that day on, the

King and the Queen were (just) man and wife, and the
people liked them very much. They were known well
after that. The King and the Queen coincidentally died
on the same day, meaning the Queen died on the same
day as the King, and the King died the same day as the
Queen, or reverse otherwise. And they died, and
everybody who was at that party, or everybody who
lived in the country came to that party . . . er . . . that
came to the funeral . . . and the people were really upset. Some of the people cried, some of the people were
sad, but they didn't think it was really worth cryin'. I
mean, you know, they were really sad, but they didn't
want to cry, and other people . . . they were kind of
glad that the King died, and those were the people
with the negative side. Those were the people that
were hated, and they took it out on the King.

So from then on, the King and Queen cherished [*sic*] off
in another world so far, far away. I mean just billions and
billions and quadrillions of miles away, zillions of miles,
etc. I mean, actually, it was just next door. The end.
*Moral: Do unto others . . . as you would expect them to do*
*unto you.*

## ANALYSIS

Sean seemed uncharacteristically quiet and self-
contained on this particular evening, in rather marked
contrast to the expansiveness of the story itself
(". . . they made super giant cakes . . . about the size of
a room," etc.). He launched into the story without any
invitation from me, which was also something of a departure for him; he usually opened our sessions with a

recital of important events at the group home or other highlights of his week. Although my immediate impression upon hearing his story was that Sean was struggling with the loss of his treatment parents, as his co-residents were, important dynamic elements established a clear parallel to other stories Sean had told me (including the diagnostic story in Chapter 2). This illustrates not only how the storytelling process highlights the periodic reappearance of a child's nuclear conflict but also how such stories furnish the clinician with an opportunity to assess the comparative success of the child's evolving adaptive strategies. My response to Sean's story follows.

---

THERAPIST'S RESPONSE
("THE KING AND THE QUEEN")

Once upon a time, there lived a King and his wife, who was the Queen. They lived in a far-off land, and this story takes place a long time ago. Well, anyway, this King and Queen began their reign when they were both pretty old, and the kingdom that they reigned in was having a lot of problems. There were all kinds of things that were going wrong with their subjects—with the people who lived in the kingdom—and they needed good and fair rulers, both a King and a Queen . . . they needed fair people to come and help them. When the King and the Queen came, they had very good intentions, and they wanted very much to help the people in the kingdom as best they could.

And, at the beginning, things went really well. They had some very high ideas of what they wanted to do. They had goals, kind of high goals of what they

wanted to achieve with the people in their kingdom.
At the beginning of their reign, when they first
started to rule, everything went really well, and people were happy, in general. But after a while, they
started to do . . . sort of strange things, and they became unpopular not only with their subjects in the
Kingdom but also with what we call the parliament,
other people who . . . made the laws and helped the
King and Queen. The King and Queen were both
pretty old; they were in their sixties.

Finally, all the problems that they were having sort of
came to a head, and the conflict became very open between the parliament and the King and Queen, and between the King and Queen and the subjects they ruled
over. The King and Queen finally announced that they
would have to leave, that they couldn't rule anymore;
they didn't feel that they were being effective. . . . They
didn't want to rule anymore, either. And so they made
the announcement to the people and to the parliament,
and everybody reacted a little bit differently. Some people were very . . . well, first they felt really rejected and
hurt, and then they became angry. Some people just became really sad and depressed and . . . some of them
cried, and some of them couldn't cry. They couldn't
bring themselves to cry because it hurt so much. And
some of the people just felt that . . . well, they'd seen so
many kings and queens that it really didn't even matter.
They couldn't care less, because there'd be another set
of rulers in a little while, and . . . so, there was a whole
range of feeling about the King and Queen leaving.

Despite a lot of the . . . negative feelings that people
had about the King and Queen leaving, they decided to

have a surprise party in the castle . . . right before the King and Queen left the kingdom. And the subjects brought all kinds of exotic and delicious foods from faraway lands, and they brought all kinds of drinks . . . of every variety: liquor, wines, and beer, juices and milk, and all kinds of things that people like to drink. And, they decided, even though they felt bad and were angry—many of them—that the King and Queen were leaving, that they'd have a party to show that they had appreciated the little period of time that the King and Queen had ruled over them.

So the King and Queen left. And at about the time they left, some of the people in the kingdom who really hadn't gotten over a lot of their feelings kind of wished in the backs of their minds that the King and Queen would die, and they had fantasies about the King and Queen dying, somehow making up for the fact that . . . in a way . . . they deserted their subjects. They left, and they hadn't finished their job. But, after a time, a lot of the subjects felt different, and they realized that those feelings—wishing that the King and Queen were dead—were pretty normal feelings to have at the time . . . that, really, the King and Queen hadn't done what they said they would. They hadn't been fair and just rulers in some circumstances, and in a lot of ways, they deserved to have the hatred and the anger of their people.

So, they may or may not have lived happily ever after. No one really knows because they left the kingdom, and they went far away, and they came back to visit very infrequently, so no one had much contact with them.

*Morals: Sometimes, even kings and queens aren't necessarily fair and just rulers, and kings and queens have problems, too, that oftentimes they can't solve themselves.*

*Under certain conditions, people sometimes feel an uncontrollable anger and hatred, and think things like "I wish the King was dead" or "I wish the King and Queen were dead because they left us and rejected us," and in some ways, that feeling is justified, but part of growing up is learning to accept that . . . kings and queens have problems, too . . . just like subjects do. I guess that's the end.*

## *Analysis and Discussion*

Sean's story is about object-loss, dramatically illustrating the whole character of the separation reaction. Separation is usually regarded as the most basic of all anxiety-generating situations, and it accounts for several of the different kinds of emotional responses evinced in the story.

Separation is portrayed in the story in a fairly dramatic way. Seeing a separation as a death corresponds more closely to the sort of reaction an infant or very young child might have (i.e., *all* separations from one's parents are permanent). The death of the King and the Queen in the story is most likely an overdetermined element in that it also represents defensive hostility ("If you leave me, then I hope you die"). The whole range of feelings and emotional responses of the people in the first story to the "coincidental" death of the King and the Queen may just as easily be attributed to the storyteller himself: "Some of the people cried, some of the people were sad, but they didn't think it was worth cryin' . . . they didn't want to cry, and other people . . . they were kind of glad that the King died, and those were the people with the negative side. Those were the people that were hated, and they took it out on the King. . . . "

In an effort to ward off his anxiety and ensuing depression, Sean employs such mechanisms of defense as projection, rationalization, and distantiation. He also attempts to convince the therapist that he bears no real or imaginary responsibility for the deaths of the King and Queen. It is the "people with the negative side" who are responsible for such monstrous thoughts, the therapist is informed. Sean's use of the dimensions of time and distance is also worthy of comment. It is almost as if he were saying, "I'm trying as best as I can to defend against the pain of yet another separation by distancing myself. I wish this had happened millions years ago, in a far-away land, and to someone else."

Sean's moral, a restatement of the "golden rule," has the effect of *undoing* some of the feelings represented earlier and, as such, introduces yet another defensive strategy. In effect, the storyteller has "taken back" the anger expressed earlier, seeking to create an impression of harmony and social desirability, however superficial. Perhaps a more fitting biblical moral for the negative affectivity that pervades this story, derived from the Mosaic code, would have been "an eye for an eye, a tooth for a tooth."

Although the group response to the departure of the treatment parents was represented undisguisedly, there was an equally clear intra-individual attempt to compensate for yet another loss. The projective nature of the storytelling technique permitted Sean a relatively safe way of giving expression to feelings about the crisis in the group home—feelings he was at first unable to discuss openly.

The therapist's story is fairly transparent, attempting simply to convey two related messages extracted from the content of the child's story. First, although as children we sometimes think of adults as having the wisdom to solve even the most difficult problems, that certainly cannot always be the case. And second, a part of growing up, however painful, is learning to accept separations and losses with equanimity and the shortcomings of others with compassionate understanding.

Later in the session Sean spoke briefly of the treatment parents' decision to leave the group home. Interestingly, he denied feeling any sadness, pain, or anger about it, despite the fact that his story had provided us with such incontrovertible evidence of the depth of his feelings about the loss. It was only some weeks later that Sean was finally able to acknowledge how upset he had been on that evening.

In the weeks and months that followed, Sean's stories exhibited a gradual progression from almost exclusive reliance on unsuccessful mechanisms for conflict resolution early in his therapy to more prominent use of adaptive, relatively conflict-free solutions as we approached the termination of his treatment, with corresponding changes in his behavior in the group home and in his capacity for modulating affects and containing his impulsivity. Sean's stories were by no means free of conflict in these later stories, although a considerably expanded repertoire of adaptive strategies, including *self-observation bordering on insight*, now enabled him to negotiate such conflicts with a greater likelihood of success.

## THE CASE OF ROBERTA

### DEPLETION DEPRESSION IN A BIRACIAL CHILD

Roberta was a bright, charming, and highly verbal child of seven and a half years when her mother first brought her in for treatment. Ms. Y. was a white professional woman in her late thirties who gave birth to Roberta, her only child, several months after ending a live-in relationship with the girl's father, a black factory worker several years her senior. Roberta had limited contact with her father, whom she saw once every two to three weeks, except on those occasions when he canceled his visits or simply failed to arrive.

Roberta was tall, fit, and extremely attractive, with curly brown hair and a light-brown complexion. Her mother brought her in for treatment principally because of escalating behavioral problems in school, where she was increasingly disruptive and uncooperative. But Ms. Y. voiced other concerns as well. Roberta had become hostile and defiant at home, seemed to fly off the handle at the slightest provocation, and frequently complained of aches and pains. She spoke of "hating" her skin color, of hating herself, and of hating black people, all of which was very troubling to Ms. Y. Roberta also freely and openly engaged in compulsive masturbation, and Ms. Y., despite her own "enlightened attitude," found that both offensive and anxiety-producing.

Roberta's acute awareness of her biracial status was clearly evident from her first production in treatment: When asked to draw a picture of her family, she depicted herself as part-black and part-white, although her father, her mother, and her maternal grandmother were all drawn in with solid colors. When asked what she would most like if she were given three wishes, she immediately stated that she'd like to be taller, she'd like everyone to have straight hair, and she'd like to have long, straight hair herself so she'd be able to have "lots of pigtails." And when, on request, Roberta drew a picture of a house and tree, she also drew a sad and lonely-looking young girl peering out from behind a narrow window. The house was drawn unimaginatively; the tree had a large hole halfway up the trunk and no branches, appearing tight and constricted.

Roberta saw herself as different and as unlikable. She felt isolated and alone. Like the tree in her drawing, she was empty and depleted. She suffered, in fact, from a "depletion depression," of which the behavioral problems and compulsive masturbation were merely symptoms. Within a short time, however, Roberta developed a considerable enthusiasm for her weekly therapeutic contacts, owing to what, in retrospect, must have been an early idealizing transference.

She told this story in an early session:

---

## ROBERTA'S STORY ("SHOELACES")

Once upon a time, there was a bird named Shoelaces. He wanted a friend to play with, but he was afraid if he had a friend, the friend would make fun of his name. He wished he didn't like shoes so much, so that maybe his mother wouldn't have named him Shoelaces. He wished he could change his name. The end.

## ANALYSIS

The unhappy bird was, of course, Roberta's personal representative in her transparent story, a poignant introduction to the narrative that Roberta would develop over the course of her treatment. Shoelaces, whom she depicted in an accompanying drawing as a large, brown bird with yellow, green, and red feathers, wished to change his name and thereby alter his identity. He was lonely and empty, and seemed convinced that, even if he were to try, no one could ever take him seriously as a friend. He was a misfit, an aberration, who blamed both himself and his mother for his sad and lonely state of affairs.

Although the story immediately and forcefully underscored the social and psychological difficulties this child associated with her biracial status, it also suggested underlying deficits in her self-structure. Roberta's bird, rather than recoiling defensively from environmental insults, seemed to feel ill-equipped *at the outset* to cope successfully with the realities of the outer world.

Several sessions later, Roberta turned a squiggle of mine into a drawing and then told this next story:

## Roberta's Story ("The Ghost Who Got Stuck in the Rope")

Once upon a time . . . Joey went down to the country.
. . . He walked around, and saw a little baby ghost who
was stuck in the rope. He couldn't put his tongue in his
mouth because the rope was too tight. Joey tried to help
the ghost, but the ghost was afraid of him. The end.
*Moral: You should be nice to a baby ghost.*

### Analysis

The baby ghost, like the bird in the earlier story,
seemed to suffer from a lack of vitality; it, too, was fearful of further damage to its self-integrity through interpersonal contact and consequently suffered great pain
and anguish. The incongruousness of a ghost being
"stuck in a rope" somehow affirms the pervasive hopelessness. This was no ordinary ghost, certainly not the
sort that would be likely to frighten anyone: Not only
shadowy and formless, it was also a highly vulnerable
spirit who desperately wanted to be able to receive
help and strength from a strong, reliable person made
of flesh and blood. The baby ghost's terror could be understood to spring from its fear of empathic failure,
mirroring Roberta's own anxiety as to the likelihood
that her selfobject needs would somehow be
thwarted—an outcome that she believed would be as
true in therapy as it had been in the rest of her life. The
ghost's gagging seemed to represent Roberta's greatest
fears of being cut off from others, from the very elements necessary for psychic survival, and also seemed

to suggest her somatic complaints, which had some-times consisted of psychogenic stomach pains and nau-sea. (The anomaly of a ghost who *couldn't put his tongue in his mouth*—an action ostensibly incompatible with gagging, anatomically speaking—could symbolize the hostile and defiant behavior of which Roberta's teacher and mother had both complained.)

With the foregoing understanding of Roberta's story-production, I told the following story in response:

---

### THERAPIST'S RESPONSE ("THE LITTLE GIRL WHO GOT STUCK IN THE ROPE")

Once upon a time, there was a little girl who felt very bad and upset inside. She felt so bad sometimes that she imagined that she was invisible, like a ghost, and that nobody noticed her or cared about her, and that no one could even see her. This made her feel very bad, even sick, as if someone had tied a rope around her neck. She felt like she was gagging and couldn't breathe very well. This was very scary for her, so she finally went to talk to someone about it. Little by little, she worked with this man to loosen the rope and to change her back into a real person, since she wasn't really a ghost at all.

### Discussion

Joey, the name of the person in Roberta's story who of-fered to help get her "unstuck" from the rope, sounds a lot like Jerry, the name by which many younger patients know me. Using this similarity as a cue, I introduced a therapist-representative in the responding story, who, unlike Roberta's Joey, was able to provide empathically attuned help to the little ghost. Together, the little ghost and the man were able to gradually restore this fragmented and shadowy creature to its true human form. Although I altered the gender of the ghost in my version with the intent of making the story less experience-remote, the therapeutic message would have been nearly as strong had I let the little ghost remain a boy.

As our treatment relationship intensified over the next several months, previously nascent features of the transference became much more prominent in Roberta's play and productions. Roberta's transference underwent several transformations and, at various times, contained elements of all three of the selfobject transferences—that is, mirroring, idealizing, and partnering (Kohut, 1984; Brandell and Perlman, 1997). A relatively stable idealizing transference gradually emerged, consistent with the notion that a developmental arrest had occurred in consequence of traumatic disappointments in the idealizing realm, rooted in Roberta's father's repeated empathic failures as an idealized parental selfobject. In other words, he proved historically unable to provide his daughter with the image of strength, stability, and enduring commitment that she desperately needed.

Roberta's next story expresses her greatest hopes and her greatest fears.

---

## ROBERTA'S STORY ("THE CREATURE FROM ANOTHER PLANET")

Once upon a time there was a creature from another planet. He came to Earth and wanted to see what the peo-

ple were like there. He said they look real different from
him because he had all kinds of colors and ears that stuck
up. The first time he met some people they said, "Oh, how
strange. He doesn't look like us." He felt unhappy because
the people didn't treat him nicely. He tried to change the
way he looked so that people wouldn't make fun of him.
People thought that he looked strange, because they had
never seen anyone who looked the way he did before. The
people said, "Let's see if you're really a person." They
thought he was wearing a disguise, but he showed them
that he wasn't. He tried to explain everything to them because he wanted to see more of Earth, but they didn't believe him. He tried to find a lawyer, but couldn't find one.
Then he saw a lawyer across the street. He told the lawyer
about why he wanted to see Earth. The lawyer believed
him, and told the people. The people had to listen to him.
Then the people shaked [*sic*] hands with him. The end.

## Analysis

Roberta's painfully acute awareness of being different so
separates her from those around her that she depicts herself as a creature from another planet. In the story, it is
only through her relationship with the lawyer, to whom
she turns out of desperation, that other people are able to
accept her. The lawyer (a therapist-representative) believes her and lends his strength and authority to her
case as an articulate and powerful advocate. The transference parallel is unmistakable here inasmuch as it is the
therapist's strength and stability that Roberta has sought
to absorb and metabolize in the transference relationship
and, ultimately, to internalize and acquire as her own.

After a period in her treatment when the therapist's presence in her stories and other productions was never very far beneath the surface, a final transformation occurred that heralded the termination phase. The personal representatives in Roberta's autogenic stories began to perform the kinds of functions previously accomplished only with the help of a selfobject (the lawyer, for instance). That change reflected Roberta's growing success, via the process of transmuting internalization, in making her own the inner strength, self-confidence, and stability she had "borrowed" until then from the therapist. The story that follows, told six weeks before her final therapy session, is an example of this phenomenon:

---

### ROBERTA'S STORY ("THE WHALE")

Once upon a time, there was a whale. He was quite large, and he had three large black spots. Most of the other whales were blue or gray—without any spots. Sometimes he felt different because not too many of them looked like him and, also, sometimes one or two of them would ask why he didn't look like them. This made him feel sad inside. He didn't listen to them because everybody's different from everybody else, and he liked how he looked. He thinks he looks nice, because it's him and he thinks he looks pretty because he's himself. Even if other people think they're prettier than him, he doesn't believe them. He believes himself.

*Moral: Being different can be good because you're special.*

This began as a therapist-initiated story and, as such, represents a departure from the usual reciprocal storytelling technique. (Recall the discussion in Chapter 1 on the use of collaborative stories.) Roberta had requested that I begin the storytelling on this one occasion. Though reluctant to make this modification because I felt unconvinced that dynamically relevant material would be generated, I decided to accede in the belief that Roberta wished to test both my sense of fairness and the limits of my empathy. However, I told her that I was willing only to begin her story; she would still need to develop it and provide an ending, a condition to which she readily agreed.

I dictated the first several sentences to Roberta, who enthusiastically printed them next to a collaborative drawing we had made of the whale with the "three large black spots." Then, Roberta completed the story. Her solution to the whale's sadness and alienation did not adhere to her earlier formula: No powerful intercessor appeared in the story to assist the beleaguered whale. Instead, the whale was able to soothe and regulate his own anxiety and to find solace in the fact that all creatures are different from each other. The whale, furthermore, was able to absorb comments from others about his unusual appearance without feeling massively injured or freakish.

In earlier variations on the same theme, Roberta's capacity for sustaining such injuries to the self was much less well developed. Because I was struck by how adaptive and healthy Roberta's story was, I offered no responding story. Instead, I simply told her how much I had enjoyed it and confessed that, on this occasion, I really had nothing to add. Roberta seemed surprised, though very pleased to hear this from me, and not at all disappointed.

At about this time, Roberta's mother reported that her daughter was no longer experiencing any behavioral difficulties at school and seemed much less defiant and angry at home. She had not complained of physical symptoms for some time. Although she continued to masturbate, she no longer did so with the same urgency or frequency; moreover, she was more readily able to honor her mother's request that she confine it to the privacy of her own room.

In view of her overall progress, a decision to terminate treatment was made at this time. Roberta expressed some ambivalence but made the observation that she didn't really "need to come in anymore"; besides, she said, she wanted to use the time to play with her friends. Growing up as a biracial child certainly contributed to Roberta's difficulties, but not nearly as much as her traumatic disappointment in her father ultimately did. Roberta's propensity to react with shame and rage to narcissistic slights, her depletion depression and anxiety, and her mercurial self-esteem were functions of impaired and deficient self-structures, themselves the product of the devitalizing absence of paternal support and strength. In this way, the selfobject failures of her father, in particular, were transmuted into her own weakness, thereby reducing her capacity for regulating her own anxiety in reaction to environmental vicissitudes. Once Roberta could begin to compensate for these structural deficits via the therapeutic relationship, she was able to repair the existing faults in her self-structures; treatment became more or less superfluous.

## STORYTELLING WITH A BORDERLINE CHILD: THERAPEUTIC CONSIDERATIONS

In working with the borderline child, the therapist is faced with various clinical and transference-countertransference difficulties not characteristically encountered in work with higher-functioning children (Chethik, 2000; Giovacchini, 1992; Mishne, 1992; Robson, 1983; Ekstein, 1966). These children are particularly challenging due not only to a range of problems in ego functioning and their notably primitive object relations but also to the characteristically pathogenic and disorganized environments in which they live. Although the treatment of children with nascent borderline personality organization has not been a focus of most of the literature on storytelling, I have found reciprocal storytelling to be quite useful in work with this difficult clinical population. There is one important caveat, however. Because borderline children tend to utilize primitive defenses and defensive strategies, some may at times experience difficulty in modulating powerful affects, even those expressed by the characters in their stories. Furthermore, these children may be more subject to internal disorganization arising from the articulation of disturbing themes and primitive intrapsychic conflicts. Accordingly, the therapist may wish to focus more exclusively or narrowly on a particular story element as a means of assisting such children in managing what might otherwise be overwhelming anxiety or other powerful affects. In fact, the therapist may even quite actively interpolate her- or himself in the child's version as a story collaborator rather than engaging in a reciprocal storytelling process. (I have done this on only a few occasions, in each instance with a highly disturbed, decompensation-prone borderline child with a very tenuous grasp on reality.)

## The Case of Harry

Harry, an unattractive, undersized ten-year-old child with poor coordination, wore thick corrective lenses with a strap so as not to lose them. He spoke with a nasal voice and often peppered his pressured speech with an inappropriate laugh and smile, which he used a little like punctuation at the end of a sentence or phrase. Harry exhibited markedly disturbed interpersonal relatedness, panic-like anxiety and occasional paranoid ideation, moderate impulsivity, a tendency toward regressive behavior, aggressive outbursts and primitive behavioral displays (e.g., kicking, biting, and urinating), and frequent shifts of mood. He also lied frequently and tended to localize all responsibility and conflicts outside of himself. He had no close friends, and his primitivity, at the levels of both affect and ideation, made him less than desirable to work with, at least initially.

Harry's mother was a severely disturbed, unstable, and highly dependent person. Recently diagnosed as borderline and manic depressive, she had been hospitalized several times during acute episodes; she was given to protracted outbursts of rage during which she remained almost completely refractory to the efforts of all around her to calm and soothe her. Harry's father was a good deal more stable and dependable, though sometimes very ineffectual in dealing with Harry's mother. Harry's involvement with him was much healthier, and this relationship became extremely important during those times when his mother was enraged, withdrawn, or hysterical.

Despite his early mistrust of the therapeutic process, which he had some difficulty differentiating from experiences at school with his teachers, Harry gradually became more comfortable in the playroom. Initially with trepidation, he also indicated that he wished to participate in story making with me, and it subsequently became a semiregular feature of our work. This is one of Harry's early stories.

---

Harry's Story

Once upon a time there was a man who was an explorer and had a ship. He lived on an island, but no one lived there with him. He was stranded. (No one was able to help him get home.) He found a hole in the earth that someone else had dug. There was a genie down there, which he saw. The genie was way, way, way down there. He was beyond the lava and all of the other rocks. The genie said he couldn't come up because of the oxygen and hydrogen in the air, but he did have assistant genies that also had magical powers. All ten of the assistant genies helped the man. All the man had to do was steer the boat. The machine-made men, who were made by the assistant genies, did everything else. The genies then went back into the hole. The man, who was in his late twenties, went back and found his parents in Pleasantville, and lived with them forever after.

*Morals: Never go out too far all alone when you explore.*

*Never go out by yourself in a far, far away place.*

## ANALYSIS

Like Derek (pp. 57–60), Harry was metaphorically suspended in what Margaret Mahler et al. (Mahler et al. 1975) called the rapprochement crisis: He was trying to move beyond the pathological relationship with his mother, but having achieved neither object constancy nor a consolidated sense of self, he lacked the intrapsychic structure to sustain his forays out into the world. Harry frequently told stories in which the protagonist (his personal representative) would venture too far and either be unable to return or face dangers that were invariably of a life-threatening sort. Here, he represented himself as the explorer who has become stranded on an island. And he represented me in a somewhat magical and idealized manner as the genie whose assistants "rescue" the stranded explorer and send him back home. I have tended to view such stories as a metaphorical equivalent for the earliest, most affectively charged experiences of exploration—that is, what Margaret Mahler has termed "practicing," or early attempts to move beyond the orbit of the symbiotic relationship. In cases of normal development, the practicing period gives way to rapprochement and to the rapprochement crisis, and, through a difficult and laborious process, finally to the consolidation of self-identity and the attainment of object constancy. But in cases involving children like Harry, for reasons that might in themselves be the topic of a lengthy presentation, neither object constancy nor a consolidated sense of self has been achieved. For several weeks, Harry had been depicting me in his stories as a genie that magically solved everyone's problems, and in my therapeutic responses, I had emphasized the limitations of the genie's "magic." Harry's compromise solution this time was to acknowledge the genie's limitations (i.e., he can't go above ground); he then, however, imbued the genie's ten assistants with the same magical and idealized transference features that had previously been associated with the genie in the earlier stories. In effect, the solution proposed in this story remains an unsatisfactory one, reflecting Harry's tendency toward massive regression to avoid panic-like anxiety associated with abandonment.

My response-story was informed by that understanding.

---

### THERAPIST'S RESPONSE

Once upon a time there was an explorer who had gone far away from home and got stranded on a desert isle. He was very, very upset and very sad because he feared he would never see his parents again. He discovered a hole, went down, and found it was very warm and dark, and there was a genie that spoke to him and made him feel much better. He asked the genie if there were assistant genies who could help him get what he needed in order to find his way back to his parents, but the genie said that both he and his assistants were powerless outside of the hole that they lived in. The man finally had to leave the hole, to search for others to help him fix his ship. He was successful, and he went back to Pleasantville, found his parents, and wanted to live with them forever. However, he also wanted to be an explorer, and decided finally to go out again with another person he had met who also liked to explore.

*Morals: It's dangerous to be an explorer only if you take unnecessary chances. As long as you follow the rules, you can explore anywhere.*

*There are no magical solutions to problems. Solving problems requires hard work.*

## Discussion

My responding story introduces the affect that is frequently isolated or otherwise primitively defended against in many borderline children. I talked about the explorer's sadness over becoming lost and his fear that he might not ever see his parents again. My explorer is frightened, although Harry's explorer never revealed his feelings. I used the symbolism of the hole, highlighting it as a retreat from the outer world where he could come to feel better, but also stressed the limitations of both the genie and his assistants. One finally must seek help and work on problems; there is no magic, nor is there someone who can do the work for you. I also tried to capture Harry's struggle over his wish to explore and his fear of annihilation. In my version of the story, the wish to explore is more powerful than the regressive retreat. There is also the intimation that one doesn't always have to explore alone; my explorer finds a partner with whom to sail his ship.

The following story, which Harry told some months later, poignantly described his difficulty in eliciting gratification from the relationship with his mother.

---

## HARRY'S STORY

Once upon a time there was an island, and a boy lived there with his father. About fifty miles away from where they lived, there was a volcano, and it was getting ready to erupt. The boy didn't know this. Another volcano was about to erupt on the other side of the island. The boy couldn't get away from either of the volcanoes, which then started to erupt. He tried to figure out how not to get hurt, and decided the only way was to dig a hole. He spent two days digging it, and on the third day, he dug out a room and rested in it. On the fourth day he started digging again, and dug back up to the surface, but he still wasn't far enough away from the volcanoes to be safe. Because of the volcanoes erupting, there were no banana trees left, and that was the main food on this island. He started digging again, and kept digging and digging, and finally he reached a cave that had lots of food that he liked to eat. He saw men in there, ancient men, but then they began to chase him. He was stuck on the island. He went all the way to the top of the island's highest mountain and saw that the volcanoes had stopped erupting. He decided to try and escape from the island, just as another

volcano started to erupt. He got on his father's speedboat, his father started the engine, and they took off.
The ancient men were still running after them, and
were very close to catching them. The father and son
didn't know, however, how to control the boat, and
then they got lost. They stopped the boat, but then
sharks circled around them; the boy's father hit one of
the sharks, and then they took off again in the boat.
But the boat flipped over and both the boy and his father drowned. The boy then woke up from his dream.
*Moral: Never run away.*

## ANALYSIS

The young person in the story is Harry's personal
representative, and the father is a paternal representative. The volcanoes, which are tremendously destructive, are a concretization of his mother's rage
and her destructive impact upon the whole family, as
well as a representation of Harry's own anger. The
boy and his father are preoccupied with both pre-
venting injury to themselves and somehow obtaining
the necessary oral supplies/gratifications to sustain
life. The father is depicted as protective and greatly
concerned for their mutual welfare, yet incompetent
and ineffectual—he doesn't know how to control his
own speedboat. In the end, malevolent forces catch
up with them both, and they are destroyed—Harry's
use of massive denial in the last line notwithstand-
ing. As stated, the moral is neither optimistic nor particularly realistic, since "not running away" is not a
viable solution, either.

Here is the story I told in response.

---

Once upon a time there was a boy who lived on an island. Sometimes the boy felt very lonely and scared, particularly when volcanoes erupted. This boy spent a lot of time trying to figure out how to stay safe and unharmed, but sometimes he would misjudge what was happening inside the volcano and it would explode, occasionally injuring him. He needed to go to the volcano area a lot because that's where the banana trees were. Even sometimes when he would try to get away from the volcano, there were still other dangers. There were ancient men who, when they saw him, would chase him. The boy's father was a very strong man whom the boy could often turn to in a time of need. The father had a boat that the boy was beginning to learn to use. Even though using a boat can be dangerous, if you learn the rules, it doesn't have to be.

*Morals: When the volcano begins to change and turn dark, stay away, and go look elsewhere for people to be with and things to do.*

*When the volcano is quiet and calm, it's okay to pick bananas.*

## Discussion

My response-story treats the volcanoes not as concretizations of Harry's rage but, rather, as a representation of his mother's "affect storms." It emphasizes the protagonist's development of better judgment and more accurate perception, and proposes a different solution to the problems of procuring "oral supplies," namely, to try and get them when Mom is emotionally available but to look elsewhere when she's too hysterical, withdrawn, or enraged. Not unlike the first story, it also emphasizes the relative safety and desirability of autonomous activities.

After over two years, Harry's treatment with me had to come to an end because I accepted a position in another part of the country; accordingly, arrangements were made for Harry to enter treatment with a clinic colleague. Harry had shown modest improvement during the latter months of our work together, although he continued to have difficulty in the management of aggression. He also continued to defend against anxiety with impulsive acting-out and a constellation of primitive defenses (regression, externalization, and projective identification). Nevertheless, his overall ego functioning demonstrated a greater capacity for containing powerful affects, as well as evidence that certain adaptive resolutions to conflict were beginning to operate alongside more conflict-laden ones. In particular, he appeared much more inclined to seek out his father and others who displayed emotional equanimity when his mother proved emotionally inaccessible or unapproachable.

Harry expressed anxiety and sadness over the termination of our work, indicating both in a story he told some three weeks prior to our termination interview:

HARRY'S STORY

Once upon a time, there was a penguin who had a problem. He couldn't swim and he didn't know how to get to the eating place. Usually, he hopped on a big animal's back, but he didn't know how to get to the eat-

ing place by himself. Then the big animal left. He
asked a penguin friend to teach him how to swim, and
the penguin friend showed him how. The friend
tapped him into the water, and the penguin thought
that he could swim. "Look here," he said, but it turned
out he was sitting on top of a killer whale. The penguin got stuck on an iceberg near the killer whale, and
the killer whale started to chop at the ice and make it
smaller and smaller. The penguin started to swim toward the shore. Well, from then on, he knew how to
swim.

## ANALYSIS

Harry's story, though cartoon-like, is a moving portrait
of his panic-like anxiety over the prospect of our treatment relationship coming to an end. Harry represents
himself as a flightless arctic bird surrounded by dangers that lurk beneath the surface. He wonders anxiously whether he will be able to obtain the necessary
nourishment from his new therapist, or whether he
will perish because he has been cut loose without having been taught the necessary survival skills by the big
animal (both myself and Harry's father). True, Harry's
avian agent survives in this story, somehow making it
to the shore in a sort of baptism by ice water. In this respect, Harry's story represents real progress, a notable
effort at individuation and autonomous action. At the
same time, the penguin friend seems a somewhat un-
trustworthy substitute for the abandoning big animal,
having led the little penguin astray. Probably both the
arctic water and the carnivorous sea life beneath its

surface represent Harry's mother, who continued to suffer from serious emotional problems of her own. They may also signify Harry's own fearful impulses and disorganizing affects, which have threatened to erupt from the depths due to his own inadequate defenses.

It was on this understanding of Harry's termination story that my response, reproduced here, was predicated.

## THERAPIST'S RESPONSE

Once upon a time, a penguin lived in the North Pole who was unable to swim and had difficulty getting to his eating place. He had gotten to know a large animal who used to help him by carrying him on his back to his eating place. One day this animal announced that he had to leave because he was moving to the South Pole, very far away. The little penguin was upset by this and became very frightened. He feared that he would be unable to get to the eating place by himself. Fortunately, the bigger animal wasn't going to be moving right away, so they were able to talk about the penguin's fears some more. The penguin, however, was still very frightened of having to swim to the eating place because he was afraid of being eaten by a killer whale. The big animal encouraged him to talk about this fear, and also reminded him that there were others he knew who would be willing to talk to the penguin about these fears, and who would make sure that he got to the eating place. The penguin was only partially reassured, however. The big animal then reminded the penguin that, even after he left, he could probably re- member things that they talked about and did with each other, and that these memories might also help the little penguin to get by in the first few weeks after the big animal went away.

There are three morals to my story.

*Morals: It can be sad and frightening when something familiar is going to change, even when most things are going to stay the same.*

*It's very important to talk about such fears and feelings.*

*Even after the big animal goes away, there are things that the penguin learned from the big animal that will help him survive.*

## Discussion

One of the first things established in my responding story was the quality and magnitude of the little pen- guin's fearful affect, hinted at but not really mentioned explicitly in Harry's version. My little penguin becomes very frightened, and this develops into an organizing motif for my response. The penguin and the bigger an- imal discuss the problem at some length, and other so- lutions are proposed. The penguin is reminded that not everything is going to change, and that there are others he knows who can help the penguin get to the eating place. Because Harry's mother continued to exert a de- structive influence on him, the danger of the arctic wa- ter with its killer whale had to remain in my version. And because the resolution does not offer empty reassurances, the therapeutic rendering is not immediately appealing or completely reassuring to the little penguin. One element that I grafted onto the responding story was the penguin's ability to summon positive affective memories of his experiences with the bigger animal to ease his panic and provide sustaining strength. This was rooted in my real confidence that Harry now had the ability to draw from a repertoire of such experiences, developed both in our treatment relationship and in his improved relationship with his own father.

## SUMMARY

In this chapter, we have explored the efficacy and versatility of reciprocal storytelling when applied to a range of clinical issues varying with respect to underlying dynamic themes, symptom severity, and the intercurrent influence of environmental factors. In the first example, the child's and therapist's stories made possible the meaningful exploration and therapeutic management, *per metaphor*, of a significant ongoing loss in the life of an eleven-year-old boy. In the second example, that of the biracial girl, reciprocal and collaborative story making proved uniquely valuable in illuminating aspects of this child's self-development and in assisting her completion of developmental tasks that had been derailed due to an earlier arrest in the idealizing selfobject realm. In the third and final vignette, reciprocal storytelling is used with considerable success to help a borderline child develop more effective ways of handling disorganizing affect states and cope with maternal pathology as well as abandonment fears. Although certain modifications of technique may be required in more severe cases, reciprocal storytelling is a potentially fertile approach even with the borderline population, often acknowledged as among the most difficult and challenging to treat (Chethik, 2000; Mishne, 1992; Robson, 1983).

# CHAPTER 5

# The Unfolding of the Narrative in the Psychotherapy of a Traumatized Ten-Year-Old Boy

Creating and maintaining the necessary therapeutic environment to enhance and cultivate the unfolding of the child's narrative account are critically important and often difficult tasks in child psychotherapy, the more so when there is a history of trauma. Under ordinary circumstances, the child develops a *narrative sense of self* during the third or fourth year of life (Zeanah et al., 1989, p. 662). Most children are capable of verbal sequencing, an important prerequisite for the construction of a narrative, by the time they turn three—that is, they can say what happens first, what comes after, and so forth—and most have the ability to use the correct tenses in referring to past and future by the age of five (Engel, 1999).

Arriving at that capacity for narrating one's own life story is therefore a "momentous achievement" (Zeanah et al., 1989, p. 662).

## Treatment Considerations

In the psychotherapy of traumatized children, however, the emergence of the child's narrative account is apt to be particularly complicated. As already observed, for the therapist to permit the child to express primitive fantasies, regressive wishes, fears, or conflicts does not suffice; he or she must extract the child's narrative from these fragmentary communications, making every effort to understand the narrative that emerges as a unique rendering of historical events. When consideration is not given to the traumatized child's narrative from the very first clinical contact, a likely effect is interference not only with the flow and content of the therapeutic discourse but with the very integrity of the intersubjective field itself, creating a climate of resistance fueled by mistrust, or perhaps one of superficial compliance. In any case, a meaningful treatment relationship fails to evolve, and in the worst-case scenario, retraumatization may actually occur. Whereas a number of techniques in dynamic child psychotherapy can serve as effective vehicles for the unwinding of a child's narrative, including a variety of representational play activities through which the clinician endeavors to create a climate of trust and to establish a vital affective tie with the child, the autogenic story can be particularly effective in eliciting a meaningful narrative from a traumatized child.[1]

The case of Nathan, vignetted next, illustrates several important aspects of the treatment process with traumatized children. First, it demonstrates how narrative dialogue evolved in the treatment of one such child and evidences the unique suitability of the autogenic story for the expression of his narrative. Second, it establishes the importance of the therapist's empathic resonance with each of the child's efforts to construct a narrative from remembered historical events. Finally, it shows how meaningful the therapist's participation in the narrative discourse can be when the autogenic story is used not solely as a vehicle for the child's narrative but also as a medium for the therapist's metaphorical communications. The reciprocal interchanges afford both participants an opportunity for powerful immersion in the traumatic experiences as recast by the child in autogenic-story form; the child's internal representations of this historical milieu are then accessible for ongoing reparative work.

## THE CASE OF NATHAN

Nathan was ten at the time of referral and lived with his adoptive mother, twelve-year-old brother, and fifteen-year-

---

[1]Storytelling has been used in conjunction with hypnosis in treating traumatized children (Rhue and Lynn, 1991). Although it is possible for this combination to enhance the treatment of certain severely traumatized children who may actually require the safety of a dissociative or altered state in order to begin the process of self-healing, the present chapter assumes a conventional, reciprocal storytelling procedure (i.e., one without hypnotic induction).

old half-sister. His principal presenting features included disorganized behavior, difficulty in modulating and expressing affects, poor impulse control, rageful outbursts, and competitiveness with his siblings. Nathan's adoptive parents had separated some six months earlier; his father subsequently announced his intention to seek a divorce, moved nearly two thousand miles away, and abruptly ceased all communication with Nathan and his brother and sister. All three children were profoundly impacted, and all became symptomatic in the wake of their parents' breakup and their father's abandonment. Such family disintegration would generate considerable upheaval even in the lives of children whose early development was quite healthy. Nathan's infancy and early childhood, however, were not. His natural mother was addicted to alcohol and several other drugs and was episodically involved in prostitution. She had a series of live-in relationships with men: Nathan and his brother were the offspring of one such relationship, which ended shortly after Nathan's birth; his half-sister was the product of an earlier liaison.

When Nathan was still an infant, his mother often left him in the care of that sister, although she was barely six years old herself. At the age of approximately two years, Nathan was forced by his older siblings into a basement room; when they left to play with friends, Nathan remained there for several hours until neighbors responded to his frantic cries for help. On at least one occasion, all three children were left for an extended period without any food; that incident led to the involvement of child protective services and, in turn, to temporary foster care. The profound maternal neglect that Nathan experienced in this highly pathogenic environment was compounded by his mother's unpredictable and occasionally abusive or even sadistic behavior. (One of Nathan's earliest memories was of being forced by his mother and his older brother to eat his own vomitus.)

Nathan was approximately two and a half when his mother was arrested for driving while intoxicated following a traffic accident. He and his siblings were in the car at the time; they watched their mother being led away in handcuffs, and that, in fact, was the last time they saw her. Nathan was placed in a series of foster homes and separated from his brother and sister during much of the two-year period preceding their adoption—a separation that must have intensified the dislocation and loss he had already experienced.

Whatever caregiving came his way in such a bleak and impoverished interpersonal environment was not attuned to his requirements for physical and emotional sustenance. Indeed, the desolate relational landscape of Nathan's environment captures the essence of the *continuous construction* model of trauma (Zeanah et al., 1989), whereby trauma must be understood relative to the context within which it occurs—and it is more likely to occur when the child is exposed to a chronic and unremitting pattern of insensitive and unattuned caregiving. This is not to deny that single, massive psychological or physical traumas exert profound and enduring effects on psychological behavior (Eth and Pynoos, 1985) but, rather, to affirm the power of traumata involving *prolonged* privation, deprivation, or psychological or physical abuse.

According to his adoptive mother, Nathan at four and a half was incapable of dressing himself, could not use eating utensils properly, and had the personal hygiene skills of a two-and-a-half- or three-year-old. He arrived without any personal possessions aside from a few articles of old clothing. Nathan and his older brother Hollis soon began to fight constantly, and Hollis, who reportedly had been sexually abused while in foster care, attempted to reenact this abuse on his younger brother. Fortunately for Nathan and his brother and sister, their adoptive mother was deeply committed to making the adoption work, even when her marriage began to fail.

Slightly above average in intelligence and reasonably verbal with a good imagination, Nathan seemed to be a good candidate for psychoanalytically oriented individual treatment. He especially enjoyed reciprocal drawing and storytelling games, techniques used frequently during the three years we worked together. The following story transcription is a verbatim dialogue derived from an interview that occurred shortly after the initial diagnostic session. Its theme of separation and abandonment was to become a very common one in the early phase of Nathan's therapy.

CHILD: Once upon a time, there was a cat and a dog and all these little children. One time, all these little children got lost. The little girl said, "We're lost! We're lost!" They seen a dog, and the dog said, "Are you lost?" They said, "Yes." Then the cat came along and said, "We'll give you a ride back to where you're supposed to be." Then they took them back where they were supposed to be, and they were happy. That's the end.

THERAPIST: Can you tell me what the story teaches us?

CHILD: It's about people getting lost and helping them, the dog and the cat helped them.

THERAPIST: So, how would you say the lesson? When you get lost, what should you do?

CHILD: Yell.

THERAPIST: Yell?
CHILD: For help.


ANALYSIS

Nathan's story is as important for what it reveals as for
what it fails to convey. The readily identifiable theme
comes as no great surprise in light of Nathan's multiple
separation and abandonment traumas. The children in
the story, however, express neither fear nor even mild
anxiety over being lost; they are simply "happy" when
returned to "where they were supposed to be." Like the
storyteller, they seem to have difficulty in experiencing,
identifying, and, ultimately, giving expression to powerful affects. Such difficulties in affectivity and in the capacity for verbalization, sometimes collectively referred
to as *alexithymia*, may be associated with *anhedonia* (the
inability to experience pleasure), or impairment in the
capacity for self-care.

This symptom constellation appears often in posttraumatic conditions, according to H. Krystal (1993). J.
McDougall (1984, 1985, 1989), expressing a similar
viewpoint, prefers the term *disaffectation* to *alexithymia*
to underscore her application of dynamic rather than
neurobiological principles to explain the mechanism
whereby a sort of psychological foreclosure of potential affects and affect representations occurs. The result
is that "certain people are psychologically separated
from their emotions and may indeed have 'lost' the capacity to be in touch with their psychic realities" (Mc-
Dougall, 1989, p. 103).

The children in Nathan's story seem unable to resolve their own problems without the use of magical
solutions: A dog and a cat appear to assess the situation and then to rescue the "lost" children. Nathan's
omission of human characters in the "rescue" is of
particular interest, for it suggests that the parents of
these lost children were not especially reliable or concerned; in fact, they are conspicuously absent from the
story. The only characters that seem to have any genuine concern for the welfare of these children are the
cat and the dog. One might say that the unspoken terror of abandonment, the ensuing state of helplessness,
and the paralysis of ego functions are all represented
in this brief account. In all likelihood, Nathan's story
recapitulates several specific traumatogenic events
that occurred prior to the age of three; at the same
time, it portrays the chronic and enduring aspects of
his early caregiving environment and a fairly primitive level of adaptation. The latter is underscored by
the noticeable failure of the story protagonists even to
seek help from adults.

As we approached the end of Nathan's first year of
treatment, the relationship had intensified, transferential features were beginning to emerge, and we
had started to engage in a very different kind of therapeutic interaction. We continued with storytelling,
though somewhat less regularly. Nathan introduced
a game in which I was a physician and he was my patient. Usually, he would be near death, generally as
the result of multiple bullet or knife wounds; he
would collapse on the floor and I would be charged

with the difficult task of resuscitating him. Coexisting with his unmistakable portrayal of the world as filled with life-threatening and malevolent forces (paralleling his own early experience) was his ability to entrust his life to another and to derive life-sustaining energy from his interaction with this human partner. This drama alternated with another scenario in which we were two African explorers: Together we would fight wildebeests, alligators, and other dangerous animals. The second play represented the therapeutic alliance itself. The two scenarios revealed Nathan's preliminary efforts to communicate the affective content and environmental context of his early traumatic experiences, his continuing fears and anxieties, as well as his belief that therapy might help him.

At the height of this activity, about sixteen months into treatment, Nathan's therapy was disrupted when I left the country for three weeks to attend an international conference. When I returned, Nathan was inconsolably angry with me: I could do nothing right, and I had "wrecked" his therapy beyond repair; my efforts to empathize with the pain and abject distress he had experienced in my absence seemed futile. The significance of the anger that he was now able to feel, identify, and express toward me was not lost—but the positive valence of the therapeutic climate rapidly deteriorated. For a time, therapy came to resemble the nightmare world of Nathan's early childhood, a place where no one seemed to care, where people disappeared and reappeared without explanation, and where it was simply too dangerous to make any kind of meaningful emotional investment.

Some two months after my return, Nathan told a story in connection with a squiggle of mine that he had turned into a picture of a broken heart. The storytelling process with Nathan during this period was framed as a "talk show," a format I had suggested and for which he had shown interest. As mentioned earlier, this vehicle can be highly effective with certain children; in addition to appealing to a child's narcissism ("And now, live from New York, it's 'Squiggles,' with our *special* guest, Nathan . . . "), it lends a certain excitement to the storytelling process. Nathan decided to play the role of the interviewer rather than the subject—a new experience for him and one that he found particularly gratifying, perhaps because it permitted him to exchange a passive position for a more active one. Nathan had seldom shown interest in listening to the playback at the conclusion of previous session tapings, but he did so eagerly on this occasion.

CHILD: This is a TV program—"Squiggles"! We have a
    guest today. What is your name?
THERAPIST: My name is Jerry.
CHILD: Glad to meet you. You gotta do a squiggle, and I
    gotta draw a picture.
THERAPIST: OK. We'll use this paper.
CHILD: Gotta close your eyes, too. It's the rules.
THERAPIST: Gotcha.
CHILD: Now I've gotta draw a picture, folks. [He draws
    the picture.] I just drew a picture of a heart because
    it's broken.

THERAPIST: A picture of a broken heart. Okay. And can you now make up a story about the broken heart, Nathan?

CHILD: Okay. Here goes.

Once upon a time there was a broken heart. He lived in the land of hearts. There was many, many hearts. He was the only one that was broken. He didn't have any friends or nobody to play with him. He just had a little house, and he just sat there, and when it's dinnertime he would eat, and breakfast . . . or lunch. . . . He went outside one day and he seen this girl. He goes, "What is your name?" She goes, "Cathy." He goes, "My name is Gary." She goes, "What happened?" He goes, "I'm shy, and I'm a broken heart. I don't have any friends."

THERAPIST: Can I just interrupt for just a second. This is a made-up story? It's not like from *Care Bears* or something? . . .

CHILD: No! I don't watch *Care Bears!*

THERAPIST: All right. But it *is* something that's made up?

CHILD: Yes!

THERAPIST: Completely original?

CHILD: Yes!

THERAPIST: Okay. So, you never heard it from anybody?

CHILD: No!

THERAPIST: All right, go ahead.

CHILD: Then he asked her some questions, and he started playing with her and stuff, and they were friends. Pretty soon he was a whole heart! He wasn't broken anymore. Every night after supper he would go over to Cathy's house and would play games with her and stuff. Then all the other hearts would play with him, too. And one day there was this heart who went home crying because *he* was a broken heart. Then Gary went up to him and says, "What is your name?" He goes "Cary." He goes, "What's the matter?" He goes, "I'm a broken heart now. I don't have any friends anymore." He goes, "Well come with me, I'll make you some friends." So he made him some friends, and . . . that's end of the story.

THERAPIST: Very good. Is there a lesson to this story?

CHILD: Don't be mean to people. . . .

THERAPIST: Don't be mean. . . .

CHILD: . . . Or else you'll break their heart. And that is the end of the program. Thank you very much for being here, Dr. J.

THERAPIST: Well, pardon me, but that is the end of the first half of the program—before our commercial break. You did want to do a commercial today, didn't you?

CHILD: Yeah.

THERAPIST: You can do two or three if you want. I'll make my story up while you do that, okay?

CHILD: Uh-huh.

ANALYSIS

Nathan told this story with considerably more feeling than I had grown accustomed to hearing in his earlier story-narratives. Although the content and tone were serious, I detected an emerging playfulness in the telling. The reversal of roles and the repartee near the beginning of his story, which we both experienced as pleasurable, would probably not have been possible at an earlier point in therapy.

Nathan's broken-heart metaphor conveyed the profound pain that multiple abandonments have caused him and, at the same time, captured the enduring desolation and emptiness of his early object world. Although the disruption in his treatment reawakened these older injuries, resulting in a mild degree of retraumatization, the story demonstrated a decidedly more adaptive effort than at any previous time in Nathan's therapy to struggle with the loneliness and despair associated with his early caregiving environment. The first broken heart, Gary, becomes a whole heart when he is able to develop a meaningful affective relationship with Cathy, a representative of the adoptive mother and the therapist. The now-restored heart is then able to establish rapport with another broken heart, Cary, at the story's conclusion.

This story signaled an important development in Nathan's treatment, inasmuch as it reflected considerable evolution of his personal narrative. Still, however, there was evidence of his tendency to employ magical solutions, and Gary's transformation via his relationship with Cathy was not elaborated to any extent. Accordingly, I responded this way:

CHILD: And now, folks, back with Dr. J. and his story.
THERAPIST: Thank you for the kind introduction. Your story was a very good one, so it's going to be a hard one to follow. But I'm going to try. Once upon a time, there was a broken heart—a broken heart who lived in the land of hearts where most of the other hearts were whole hearts. Well, this broken

heart was broken for a number of reasons, but especially because of the things he had lost—mostly the people he had lost. He was very sad. He was very depressed and very lonely, and felt very bad inside. Furthermore, there never seemed to be anyone for him to play with. There were hardly any people around near his little house in the little part of town in which he lived.

Well, one day he left his little home in the land of hearts, and he went to live with a family of whole hearts who lived on the other side of the village. It wasn't easy to move in with this family of whole hearts. At times, he still felt really lonely and really depressed and sad. But, little by little, the broken part of him started to mend. But it took a very long time. After a while, though, he began to feel loved. He also began to feel loving toward other hearts—something that he hadn't been able to do for a long time, because he hadn't been able to trust other hearts very much 'cause of how he had been hurt. But everything didn't always go smoothly. Sometimes things were really hard, and sometimes he got into fights, or people yelled at him or he yelled at them. He even felt hatred toward the whole hearts, and felt that they hated him. But those times became fewer and further between, and he felt more and more whole, as he lived with this family of whole hearts. He was even able to give friendship and love toward another broken heart one day when he was called on to do that. And that's the end of the story. It is a story that continues, but that's the end.

There are two morals. The first is: *Becoming a healed heart takes time and hard work.* And the second moral is: *When you feel whole, then you can begin to give to other people, too—or, in this case, to other hearts. And that also takes time, but it's possible.* That is the end of my story.

CHILD: Thank you for being on the show, Dr. J. We'll see you next week.

## Discussion

My version of Nathan's story attempted to develop four interrelated themes. One was that a broken heart becomes broken for compelling reasons: Sadness, depression, and loneliness are the sequelae of the painful losses that the broken heart has suffered. A second was that there is, indeed, cause for optimism about the broken heart mending, although such healing takes a long time and requires hard work. The third message was designed to counter the idealized quality of the healing process as it was represented in Nathan's story by asserting that there will still be times when the mended heart reexperiences injury, depression, sadness, or even hatred, but also that such feelings are part of daily living. Finally, the notion that trust and empathic rapport are indeed possible for a mended heart was implied in the therapeutic response, although it was less central there than in Nathan's version.

As the third year of therapy began, Nathan continued to show improvement both in his capacity for modulating and expressing affects and in his ability to control his impulses. His interpersonal skills gradually improved and his performance at school remained strong. He also began to address issues at the core of his traumatic past both through play metaphors and in direct verbal discourse.

The last pair of stories comes from a session conducted at about the time we began the termination process, well into the third year of treatment.

CHILD: Once upon a time, there was a rabbit. The rabbit was white. One day a girl found this rabbit in the woods. The rabbit was hurt very badly because it got chewed up by some hunting dogs. The dogs chewed some of the rabbit's skin off. So, the little girl took the rabbit home and took care of it until the rabbit got better. Then the girl let the rabbit go. Then it was all better. One year later the girl was going to school. The girl saw the rabbit at her house. When the girl's father saw the rabbit, he started shooting at it. The rabbit ran and ran and ran. Then the girl was really mad because she thought the rabbit was dead. Then one winter, the girl was going to school. She was walking to school, and she saw the rabbit. She didn't think it was the rabbit because it didn't look white. It was very hungry. So the girl gave the rabbit some carrots to eat so it could be healthy again. And they lived on.

The moral of the story is: *Help animals and people, even if you don't know them.*

ANALYSIS

Not only well constructed but also told with a range of powerful affects including anger, sadness, and despair, this story displays the dramatic transformation of Nathan's personal narrative over the course of treatment. Nathan had become far more expressive and was now possessed of a maturity that made him seem much older than the fragile and helpless child I first welcomed to my office some three years earlier. The rabbit is, of course, his personal representative, traumatized by a series of vicious attacks and abandonment. The girl represents the adoptive mother and, to a lesser degree, the therapist; the girl's father is the abandoning adoptive father, whom Nathan experienced in real life as inhuman, insensitive, and cruel. The moral of the story is a particularly interesting one, inasmuch as it suggests the process not only of adoption but also of psychotherapy.

The chief source of concern about this story, an otherwise quite adaptive one, was the choice of a rabbit as a personal representative. I tend to view rabbits as exquisitely sensitive but usually mute creatures. Even if they become injured or feel strongly about something, they may be quite limited in their ability to express this. Therefore, I believe Nathan's choice of this animal was not a coincidence but, rather, reflected both its vulnerability and its muteness. In any case, the rabbit's need for time and space in order to come to terms with its past—and, finally, to be capable of accepting help from the girl—isn't developed to any great extent, thus also imparting a somewhat magical and unrealistic quality to the story's resolution. These thoughts influenced the composition of my responding story:

THERAPIST: Once upon a time, a girl found a rabbit in the woods where she had been playing. The rabbit had been very badly hurt. He was seriously injured and very scared. He was also very lonely and was very afraid of people and dogs and just about everything. He couldn't talk and wasn't able to tell the girl everything that had happened to him, although she seemed to know some of the things without his even having to say them. She took the rabbit home and began to care for him. His wounds began to heal and he began to eat again. He gained some weight because he had been awfully skinny when she first found him.

After a while, although the rabbit liked the girl, he wasn't really able to trust her completely, and he decided he wanted to leave. The girl understood this and let him go. For a long time she never saw him or heard about him, and she missed him very much. The rabbit also missed her, because here was someone who had really been good to him, maybe for the first time ever. The rabbit endured some very bad hardships; some very unpleasant things happened to him during the year he was away, and he began to miss her very much.

One day when the girl was coming home from school she saw the rabbit. He was skinny, so thin you could almost see through him. His eyes were almost popping out from all the weight he had lost, and he was dirty and looked very unhealthy. The girl immediately picked him up and, because she loved him so much, brought him home again to care for him. The rabbit went home and was very happy to be there.

Well, something very unexpected happened. A man who lived next door to the girl, who didn't understand anything about this rabbit, one day saw the rabbit, and took out his hunting rifle. He loaded the rifle and was about to shoot it. Suddenly the rabbit lifted up its head and screamed at him, "Don't shoot me"—of course, in a higher voice. The man was startled and didn't know what to do. In amazement he put down his gun and stared at this rabbit that had spoken to him. The rabbit stared back and repeated, "Don't hurt me!" The man was so amazed that, shaking his head, he turned away and walked home. The girl returned from school a bit later that day. The rabbit told her what happened. The girl was less amazed that the rabbit could speak than the man had been, because she had understood a lot about him without his having to speak about it before. But, because he was able to speak, he was finally able to tell the girl much more about himself—about all the problems he had had, about the hardships he had suffered, and about many other things that weren't especially bad or frightening, too. So the girl understood him better and better all the time. She continued to care for him. And, because she was able to care for him so well, the rabbit learned how to care for himself better. He learned how to feed himself when he was hungry and to tell people about his feelings when they were important and needed to be expressed. That was a kind of healing, too. It went on for a rather long time, almost until the rabbit was full-grown. And that's the end of the story.

CHILD: What's the moral?

THERAPIST: There are two morals to this one. The first is: *Some wounds never heal completely. They heal pretty much, but they're never completely healed, and they leave scars. But, in time, with love and patience and nurturing and understanding, a rabbit or any creature can begin to feel whole.*

And the second moral is: *When somebody does something to you that's painful, that hurts you, or that makes you feel bad, let them know, like the rabbit did. Tell them, "Don't hurt me." And if they won't listen, find someone who will. That's the end.*

## Discussion

The responding story expands on the relationship between the girl and the rabbit. The girl, like Nathan's adoptive mother, understands that trust in a relationship must evolve gradually and that there are occasional setbacks. The man whom Nathan designates as the girl's father (representing the adoptive father) is a peripheral character in my version, principally because he was clearly out of the picture by this time. Providing the rabbit with the faculty of speech went a long way toward making him less reliant on others; it also demonstrated the power of self-expression. Despite the fact that my story was somewhat longer than his, Nathan remained intently focused and interested in it from beginning to end. Some sort of synchronicity prevailed between us that made this exchange of stories feel as though we had experienced a shared altered state. This session with Nathan probably came as close as any I have known before or since to capturing the enchantment and power of storytelling as a narrative device.

Like the rabbit in his story, Nathan gradually developed a capacity for basic trust and began the process of healing. His personal narrative, though incomplete, demonstrated a richness and cohesiveness that stood in marked contrast to earlier versions of his "story" from the first weeks and months of therapy.

## SUMMARY

This chapter has explored reciprocal storytelling in relation to the treatment of a traumatized child, spotlighting the continuous construction model of trauma. An extended clinical vignette illustrates the process of psychotherapy with an alexithymic ten-year-old boy who had been subjected to multiple traumas. One key theme is the evolution of the narrative discourse with this patient over the course of therapy; another is the contribution of therapeutic storytelling in that evolution.

# CHAPTER 6

# Transference Dimensions of the Storytelling Process

D uring the past fifteen years, contemporary psychoanalysis has been in a state of sustained excitement and controversy. A series of significant developments in both psychoanalysis and psychoanalytically oriented psychotherapy has, cumulatively, led to conceptualizations of practice that sometimes appear to be at striking variance with more traditional distillations of theory. As it happens, much of this ferment seems related to transformative shifts in our understanding of elemental aspects of the relationship in psychoanalysis and psychoanalytic psychotherapy. Our views of the clinical process, particularly as it is shaped by our understanding and clinical management of transference and counter-transference phenomena, is at the heart of this theoretical debate.

Child treatment issues are a focus of only a small proportion of the voluminous psychoanalytic literature of the last decade and a half. Nevertheless, this literature reflects core changes in our understanding of the psychotherapeutic process in child psychoanalysis and child psychotherapy, with relational issues figuring in quite prominently. Traditional views of the curative process in child analysis had mandated that the therapist verbalize conflict-laden issues as these came to be revealed in the child's play; as a consequence, such conflicts became accessible to consciousness and could be acknowledged by the child, ultimately leading to enhanced self-awareness and insight (Fraiberg, 1965). J. A. Yanof (1996) notes, however, that child analysts have paid increasing attention to the relational matrix in child analysis, with correspondingly less emphasis on interpretation as a principal medium or agent of change.

The classical assumption that interpretation need be a prominent focus of child analytic technique has been questioned for two reasons. First, as child analysts have focused increasingly on the developmental function of play in the context of child treatment, some have concluded that play as a process independent of interpretation may itself promote change and growth (Abrams, 1993; Cohen and Solnit, 1993; Neubauer, 1993, 1994; Yanof, 1996). This idea is, of course, not a novel one; it has its modern origins in the pioneering work of developmentalist and child analyst Erik Erikson (1959, 1977) and was recognized by the poets long before that.[1] Second, child analysts and therapists

---

[1] As William Blake once wrote, "The Child's Toys and the Old Man's Reasons Are the Fruit of the Two Seasons" (as quoted by Erikson, 1977).

have gradually become more involved in working with a nontraditional clientele consisting of children suffering from moderately severe, long-standing, and complex psychosocial problems (e.g., those associated with nascent disorders of character, traumatization, patterns of familial violence, and drug use). P. Fonagy and M. Target (1998) have summarized a number of recent research studies that seem quite convincingly to argue against the use of interpretations of unconscious conflict (especially of a deep or genetic nature) with these children. Not only do such interpretations generally fail to promote insight; they may actually lead to persecutory reactions or be experienced as intrusive or seductive (Fonagy and Target, 1998). Play seems both mutative and sufficient without interpretation in work with such developmentally arrested or ego-impaired children, according to several authors (Yanof, 1996; Cohen and Solnit, 1993; Neubauer, 1993). At the same time, play—which of course encompasses the making of stories, reciprocal and otherwise—does not occur in a relational vacuum; it is subject to a host of influences including, though not limited to, the forces of transference and countertransference.

## HISTORICAL AND CONTEMPORARY PERSPECTIVES

The nature, intensity, and technical handling of transference themes and reactions in child analysis and child psychotherapy have formed the basis of a protracted and passionate debate that began nearly seven decades ago. Melanie Klein (1932) and Anna Freud

(1929, 1946, 1965) were the first analysts to publish theoretical and clinical papers on the application of psychoanalytic techniques to clinical work with children. Their ideas about child development and child analytic technique were, however, radically different and led to the founding of two distinct schools of child treatment.

Melanie Klein (1932) maintained that children could be analyzed through direct interpretation of their play, which she took to be the equivalent of the adult patient's free associations. Her contention was that children were analyzable and capable of developing "a transference neurosis analogous to that of grown-up persons" (p. xvi). Anna Freud (1929) originally believed that children were incapable of forming transferences due to their ongoing relationships with their parents, whose continuing influence as primary objects was seen as an insurmountable obstacle. However, she later modified this early position, acknowledging that children were not only capable of forming transferences but might also experience reactions analogous to the adult patient's transference neurosis (A. Freud, 1965; Yanof, 1996). Nevertheless, Miss Freud continued to insist that important differences (e.g., those involving the dimensions of globalization, duration, and resolution) do exist between the child's transference neurosis and that of the adult (A. Freud, 1965; Altman, 1992; Yanof, 1996).

Current thinking about transference issues is no less complicated today than it was for child analysts and therapists practicing in the early days of child treatment. P. Tyson (1978) and J. Sandler et al. (1980), who have written extensively about transference phenomena in child treatment, consider transference in children and adolescents to fall along a continuum that includes both transference proper and transference-like phenomena (categorized as *externalizations projected onto the analyst, transferences of habitual modes of relating, transferences of current relationships,* and *transference proper*). Many writers (e.g., Chused, 1988, 1992; Abrams, 1993; Fonagy et al., 1996) are in general agreement today that children can and do experience transference reactions, that a thorough understanding of transference themes and issues is essential to effective child psychotherapy, and that the systematic analysis of transference is central to effective child analytic work (Yanof, 1996).

There seems little reason to believe that children's autogenic stories are any less likely than other kinds of metaphorical play communications to contain important manifestations of transference attitudes and feelings. Nevertheless, there has been relatively little attention given to the recognition and handling of transferential material in children's stories.[2] Both R. Gardner (1977, 1993) and N. Kritzberg (1975) have described the various ways in which children represent the therapist in story creations. Each has also provided illustrations of how therapist representations

---

[2]P. Tyson and R. Tyson (1986) have actually questioned whether interpretations of any kind that are made via displacement can be considered to have legitimacy in psychoanalytically oriented treatment. Others, however, have found such therapeutic communications to be of inestimable value, particularly in work with more disturbed children and adolescents (cf. Ekstein, 1966).

may be used to advantage in the therapist's efforts to assist the child in exchanging maladaptive or conflict-laden solutions for healthier, more adaptive and relatively conflict-free resolutions. Yet, apart from these examples, transference issues are typically not considered in any depth in the extant literature on therapeutic storytelling beyond the more general contribution they may make to the clinician's overall understanding of a given child. *Systematic interpretation* of transference via story metaphors is rarely discussed.[3]

## THE CASE OF MATTIE

### AN ILLUSTRATION OF A SELFOBJECT TRANSFERENCE

Mattie was a ten-year-old Caucasian child who resided with his mother, two younger sisters, and his mother's live-in boyfriend. He was referred by his pediatrician and school counselor, who catalogued the following complaints: secondary encopresis and enuresis; compulsive stealing from his mother's purse and, more recently, from merchants; other antisocial behavior, such as throwing things, injuring younger children (particularly his sisters), firesetting, and breaking of small objects; and, in general, poor impulse control and affect containment. Mattie's mother, Ms. R., was quite concerned that Mattie expressed no remorse over such incidents, even when confronted directly.

---

[3]Kritzberg's *structured therapeutic game method* is one of the few exceptions to this general rule, although transference interpretations using this method tend to be rather formulaic, may or may not be based on the child's metaphors, and are often therapist initiated (i.e., not in direct response to the child's story).

Ms. R. appeared to be much older than her twenty-eight years, partly in consequence of her depressive demeanor and obesity. She revealed in an early interview that she had been hospitalized several times for acute suicidal depression, most recently just before Mattie began treatment with me. Her parents had both suffered from manic-depressive disorder or perhaps depressive psychosis; both had also attempted suicide, and her mother shot herself when Ms. R. was nine years old. She described both parents as alcoholic besides.

Mattie's father, Mr. R., had succumbed to lung cancer and emphysema at the age of sixty, three years prior to Mattie's referral to the psychotherapy center. Mattie was reported to have been very close to him and profoundly affected by his terminal illness. Mr. R.'s father had committed suicide via ligature when Mr. R. was a youth, and, according to Ms. R., his mother died soon afterward from "natural causes." In addition to Mattie and his sisters, Mr. R. had two children from a previous marriage.

When Mattie was a year old, his parents left him for a week to go on a belated honeymoon. On at least five subsequent occasions, Mattie was cared for by others due to the birth of his younger siblings and his mother's psychiatric decompensations. Protective Services had become involved twice; when Mattie was three, he and one sister were briefly placed in foster care. Ms. R. freely admitted to tremendous child-rearing difficulty with Mattie. She disciplined him inconsistently, the discipline often bordering on physical abuse.

Within six months of his father's death, Mattie rode his bicycle across a busy intersection and was hit by a truck. He sustained a serious closed-head injury, which left him with minor residual left-sided weakness that was particularly noticeable when he performed certain fine-motor tasks. (The possible parasuicidal meaning of the accident had evidently not been considered by any of the medical personnel involved in his treatment.)

In our early individual interviews, Mattie seemed easily distracted and exhibited what appeared to be a quasi-startle response. He was unable to explain why he had come to see me, nor was he able to remember my name after I had introduced myself twice. He recounted a dream from his sixth year; the manifest content, which he related rather matter-of-factly, seemed to capture three salient dynamic themes that resonated throughout the other history I had already obtained.[4] In the dream, "[his] mother ate too much ice cream and she exploded." The salient elements included Mattie's rageful anger at his mother for her chronically neglectful, abandoning attitude as well as her punitive treatment of him, and also Mattie's awareness that his mother may well be an active agent in her own demise and that she is very needy. In fact, one might argue that there is very little distortion in Mattie's perception of this parent with her insatiable needs and primitive oral greed and dependency.

Treatment—psychoanalytically oriented play therapy (using such modalities as clay modeling, drawing, board games, Lego® play, doll play, sociodrama, and reciprocal storytelling)—was begun on a twice-weekly basis and continued without significant interruption for approximately

---

[4]Dated as it was, and introduced without benefit of the dreamer's associations, this dream still had presence as a source of clinical data comparable in significance to that of an early memory. One may, moreover, be guided by Freud's (1900) observation that the manifest content of young children's dreams often coincides with their latent meaning, reflecting relatively undisguised wish-fulfillment.

fourteen months, at which point the case was transferred to a colleague because I relocated to another part of the country. Gradually, it seemed reasonable to conclude that Mattie's problems grew out of arrested development. He had been subjected to an unending series of traumatic experiences that included actual parent loss, chronic psychological and episodic physical neglect, threatened parent loss through (his mother's) multiple suicide attempts, and life-threatening injuries. He lived in a relational climate devoid of vitality, where he was treated punitively and then periodically abandoned without warning. Mattie clearly suffered chronic, traumatic disappointments involving the developmental experiences of idealizing and partnering, associated with two of the three basic selfobject realms (idealized parent imago and alter ego). It is likely, if less directly evident from the clinical data, that his mother, owing to her own depressive illness, was also not reliably available to meet his developmental needs for empathically attuned mirroring, associated with the third structural domain (the grandiose-exhibitionistic self).

Mattie enjoyed pretending that he was a celebrity guest on a television talk show who told stories and performed for a vast television audience. I usually played the part of the host, although from time to time Mattie would request that we exchange roles. The story reproduced here, which was transcribed from a tape recording, dates from his fourth month of treatment. Its content foreshadows important developments in Mattie's evolving transference relationship with me; similar representations of transference were subsequently incorporated into other stories he would tell, as well as into other imaginative play activities.

## "The Wreath That Hung on the Door (That Somebody Stole)"

THERAPIST: Yes. And now, without further delay, let me turn the show over to Mattie, who has prepared a very interesting story for us. Mattie, it's all yours.

CHILD: OK, here we go. "The Wreath That Hung on the Door."

Once there was a wreath. This kid found it. He didn't know what to do with it. So, he decided to hang it on his door. He hanged it on his door one day, and then he looked out there at the wreath, and he said, "OK! Looks perfect!" So, he kept it there. Then this big bully came along, and he saw this wreath and he goes, "That's my wreath!" because he lost it and everything. So then he goes up and tries to grab the wreath. Then the boy comes out and he says, "Hey! That's my wreath!"

THERAPIST: What's the boy's name?

CHILD: Which one?

THERAPIST: The first boy—the one who has the wreath.

CHILD: Charlie.

THERAPIST: And what's the bully's name?

CHILD: Dominic.

THERAPIST: OK. Go ahead. Charlie came out and he said, "Hey! That's my wreath!"

CHILD: "That's my wreath!" And he goes, "No, it's not! It's *mine!* I lost it!"

THERAPIST: That's what Dominic said.

CHILD: Yeah. Then they started to fight over it. Then his mom came out and said . . .

THERAPIST: Whose mom came out?

CHILD: Charlie's.

THERAPIST: OK.

CHILD: . . . came out and said, "Why are you boys fighting?" "He stole my wreath!" "No, he didn't." "Yes, he did!" "No I didn't, Mom! It's true!"

THERAPIST: I'm not quite sure I'm following you now. Charlie's mom came out and said, "Why are you boys fighting," and then what happened? Now make sure you tell me who says what, because otherwise I won't know.

CHILD: Well, Dominic says, "It's my wreath. He stole it from me!" And Charlie goes, "No it's not!" And then his Mom says, "Is that your wreath laying over there?"

THERAPIST: To whom?

CHILD: Dominic. And he goes, "Yeah! That's it! Yeah! Thanks, Mrs. Evans." So he goes to pick it up, and they lived happily ever after. The end. But there's something else to that story. They said "sorry" to each other, and they made up, and they were best friends in the whole wide world. The end.

THERAPIST: OK. What is the lesson for this story?

CHILD: Don't know. Can't blame something on everybody. . . . Like suppose you think a kid stole my picture because you had exactly the same thing. Then somebody says, "Is that your picture laying over there?" So, it's like you can't blame it on everyone else.

THERAPIST: Okay. That's a good story, Mattie. Let's stop the tape recorder, and I'll get my story ready to tell back to you.

Analysis

Mattie's story is richly evocative of several aspects of a selfobject disorder or a disorder of arrested development. It captures his futile efforts to seek out meaningful selfobject experiences, his inevitable disappointment when thwarted in satisfying partnering and idealizing needs, and his efforts to diminish this pain. Like many stories told by children in therapy, it undoubtedly contains multiple meanings—yet that overdetermination in no way dilutes the transference meaning of the efforts of the protagonist (Dominic) to procure something of value from Charlie.

From the perspective of selfobject theory, Mattie's regressions in toileting, his antisocial behavior, and his impulsivity are most meaningfully understood as products of a *disintegrating self* (Tolpin and Kohut, 1980). Like his character Dominic, Mattie is unable to imagine a relationship in which the acquisition of material possessions ("things") is secondary in importance to the experience of doing and being with an attuned human partner. The subjective experience of sustained inner vitality and harmony of the self is, analogously, therefore not a part of Mattie's structural repertoire. In Mattie's desolate and empty selfobject world, human contacts are sought only to assuage painful inner depletion and disharmonious self-states. To ask for more from his overburdened and chronically depressed mother is far too dangerous, carrying with it the risk of abandonment and perhaps abuse.

In a sense, Mattie represents aspects of himself in both story characters. Although my responding story identifies Dominic as his personal representative, Charlie's dilemma is by no means unfamiliar to Mattie: A more powerful adversary lays claim to something of value that Charlie has discovered—just as Mattie's mother's selfobject needs certainly rivaled those of her son.[5] This understanding of the original story presupposes a very different basis for the transference and carries with it the possibility that Mattie will ultimately find himself in competition with the therapist, yet another unattuned and unempathic adult with his own agenda. Had this been my perspective, my focus would have been much more on Charlie and his emotional reactions, and less so on Dominic. I would have elaborated on Charlie's efforts to establish ownership over what legitimately belongs to him, as well as on his presumed distress over the prospect of the wreath being wrested away. Although I might also have reshaped Dominic's character in my story-response, making him less domineering and thuggish, and more amenable to Charlie's influence, Charlie's sensibilities, wishes, and prerogatives would have been consistently in the foreground. In this alternate scenario, the essence of the therapeutic communication is that not everyone is as needy or entitled as Mattie's mother, and that not all relationships need be cast in adversarial terms—in short, that it is possible in human relationships to achieve mutual respect and understanding.

---

[5]One might also hypothesize that sibling conflicts and competition for scarce psychological resources are represented in the conflict between Dominic and Charlie.

Yet another possibility presents itself, particularly if one assumes my rather insistent focus on the morals in the discussion following the story-response to be, at least in some measure, countertransference-driven. In contradistinction to the first two possibilities, one might instead hypothesize that Mattie's painful experience of his mother's misattunement and psychological unavailability is paralleled in the environmental response to Dominic's excitement over "discovering" the wreath. Because he is not believed, Dominic is forced to settle for a "substitute" wreath, while Charlie's interests are essentially protected by the intercession of his mother. If, indeed, Mattie's "forgetting" of the morals was dynamically motivated, it may reveal a disjunction occurring in consequence of my having "taken" his story and altered it, thereby depriving Mattie of a source of creative pleasure. In effect, Mattie and I might have unwittingly recreated in the transference-countertransference an aspect of this faulty mirroring.

Because I believed Mattie's selfobject requirements to be most consonant with the first interpretation described above, I fashioned my story-response accordingly. My decision was partly based on earlier stories and other clinical data in which the partnership theme was dominant, but it was also based on Mattie's enthusiastic narration of Dominic's lines. In this story, at least, Mattie seemed more identified with Dominic than with Charlie. Moreover, as regards both the second and third possibilities, the emerging transference configuration during this phase of Mattie's treatment (later to become dominant) also seemed closely tied to unrequited partnering and idealizing needs; his needs for affirmation or mirroring were not as clearly manifest at the time this story was told. Finally, although Mattie sometimes commented on the differences between our stories, his characteristic reaction was that of narcissistic pleasure: Invariably, his story came first, and my story, just as predictably, bore a close resemblance to it. Although this observation does not invalidate either alternate hypothesis, it suggests a stronger clinical basis for the particular route chosen: the transferential significance of Dominic's efforts to procure vital partnering and (secondarily) idealizing selfobject supplies from Charlie.

What follow are my story-response and the revealing post-story dialogue in which Mattie and I then immediately engaged.[6] Some comments on a few of the structural dimensions of my story-response may also be useful. Because Mattie was rather distractible and exhibited other problems that may have reflected mild deficits in neurocognitive functioning, my story is intentionally repetitive; morals, too, are iterated and interpreted to ensure that Mattie could absorb, assimilate, and internalize the messages.

"The Boy Who Found a Wreath
and the Boy Who Wanted a Wreath"

Therapist: OK. Now it's my turn to tell a story back to you. It's called . . . "The Boy Who Found a Wreath and the Boy Who Wanted a Wreath." OK. Once

---

[6]As mentioned earlier, such discussions at the conclusion of a story are useful both because they furnish the therapist with an opportunity to test the child's understanding of the story themes and resolutions and because they help provide a natural segue to other play activities.

upon a time, there were two boys. One was named Charlie, and the other was named Dominic. Does that sound familiar?

CHILD: Uh-huh.

THERAPIST: Well, Charlie found a wreath in an alley. It was a wreath that he pretty much figured didn't belong to anyone else because it had been carelessly tossed near the garbage cans in the alley in back of where he lived. Since he'd found it there, he decided that he might as well take it back with him. He dusted it off and cleaned it up a bit. Then he put it on his front door where other people could see it because he felt very proud of it. It really was a very pretty wreath; it was green and red, and it had special decorations on it that made it unusual, unlike the other wreaths in the neighborhood. Well, along came Dominic. Dominic was known in the neighborhood as a bully. He picked on little kids. He would beat them up, and he seemed not even to care when he did it. He could be real mean and nasty, and had a reputation for being very unfriendly and cruel. . . . Well, he saw that wreath, and he knew that it was a new wreath, one that had just been put up. He went right up to the door, and he said to himself, "I *want* that wreath. It's really neat-looking. It's really pretty. I really need something like that. I don't have one. I think I'll take it." He opened the screen door and he started to take the wreath off. Well, just as he started to take it off the door, Charlie happened to be walking by the window in his living room, and he saw Dominic. He ran to the door, and he opened the door and caught Dominic right in the act. He said, "Hey! You can't take that wreath off my door! That belongs to me! I found it!" Dominic said (even though he knew it wasn't his wreath), "No! That's my wreath! I lost it! You must have stolen it! Yeah. That's my wreath, and I'm gonna take it back!" Charlie said, "That really isn't your wreath, because someone put it in the garbage in back of my house, and I'm sure that if it were your wreath, it would have been somewhere else—not lying by the garbage in my alley." Well, they started to argue. They argued for a little while, and finally Charlie said, "Listen, Dom. I'm not going to give you the wreath because it really belongs to me. But I'll tell you what I'm willing to do. I'm willing to go with you and see if we can find another wreath that you like." Dominic sort of went like this [mimes a "double-take"]. He said, "Hey, are you kidding?" Charlie said, "No, I'm not kidding. I mean, I guess you want a wreath real bad, and even though I can't give you this wreath because it's mine, I'd be willing to go with you and try to find another one. We could look in the alley, and . . . spend some time looking in other neighborhoods to see what we can turn up." Dominic said, "Say, you're not kiddin', are you? You're serious! You serious?" Charlie said, "Yeah, I'm serious. I'm willing to do it. I've got some time . . . an hour or two now. Why don't we go?" Dominic said, "Hey Charlie, you're not such a bad guy after all. All right, Charlie . . . or can I call you 'Chuck'?" Charlie said, "Yeah, you can call me Chuck. That's what my friends call me. Let's go. Let's see what we can do." So off they went. They didn't find another wreath, but you know something? It didn't matter too much, because they had a good time; Dominic enjoyed Charlie's company, and Charlie could see that Dominic really wasn't such a terrible guy underneath, after all. There was really more to him than . . . the cruel and mean bully he had heard about in the neighborhood. So, they spent a few hours together that day, and they began to play with each other pretty regularly after that. Now, there are two morals to my story. The first one is: *Sometimes people become bullies because inside they feel real small and afraid and weak.* That's the first moral. The second moral is: *Sometimes people think they want a glittery, pretty-looking toy or something fancy, because inside they feel empty. What they really want is to feel understood*—like Dominic (in my story), who really wanted to be understood. He wanted to feel close to someone. That's why Charlie's offer of friendship was even more important to him than getting a wreath. That's why they forgot about the wreath after they spent a few hours together. That's the end of my story. But now I want to ask you what you think the biggest difference between your story and my story was today?

CHILD: The biggest?

THERAPIST: The biggest difference . . .

CHILD: Everything.

THERAPIST: Well, tell me more. What's first?

CHILD: Charlie's mom didn't come out.

THERAPIST: . . . Yeah. Charlie's mom wasn't in my story at all.

CHILD: . . . But the biggest difference is when they were fighting over the wreath, Charlie said, "I'll go help you look for a wreath in the alley." That's the biggest.

THERAPIST: Uh-huh [pause]. Well, how about this difference: Did Dominic really *lose* a wreath in this story?

CHILD: No.

THERAPIST: No, he just made that up, right? 'Cause he wanted that wreath. . . .

CHILD: Lied.

THERAPIST: He lied, yeah, 'cause he wanted the wreath that was on Charlie's door. And why did he lie in my story?

CHILD: Cause he was a big bully like he was in my story.

THERAPIST: Uh-huh. But he also thought that the wreath would make him feel neat and good inside because it was so pretty and had so much decorative stuff on it. He just wanted it real bad. He was jealous of Charlie. So, that's another difference. . . . Let's talk about the morals in the stories. The moral in your story was what, Mattie? [pause] Do you remember the moral in your story?

CHILD: Can't blame something on somebody else that didn't do it.

THERAPIST: Right. . . . And what about the morals in my story. Remember what they are?

CHILD: I forgot.

THERAPIST: Well, one of the morals had to do with being a bully. Is a bully a strong person who feels good inside?

CHILD: No.

THERAPIST: What is a bully?

CHILD: He's a jealous person.

THERAPIST: He's jealous, that's right. What else is a bully?

CHILD: Mean.

THERAPIST: Right. And why is he mean?

CHILD: Because everybody else has got something he doesn't got.

THERAPIST: Yes. He thinks that people have things that he doesn't have, and he feels weak and empty and jealous, like you said, and *small*. He feels small, even though he looks big to other people. And do you remember the other moral?

CHILD: Uhh . . . I forgot.

Well, it was a moral that had to do with people wanting things. . . .

CHILD: People wanting things . . . but I can't remember.

THERAPIST: They want things because they feel empty inside and they think that by getting fancy toys or wreaths . . . that this will fill them up and make them feel better. But, of course, it doesn't work that way. Did you like the stories today?

CHILD: Yes!

THERAPIST: They were fun, huh? You did seem like you were listening pretty closely to my story.

CHILD: [Pauses for a moment]. All right, Chuck!

THERAPIST: Okay, Dom!

CHILD: Bye!

THERAPIST: And bye to our television audience . . . until next week.

## Discussion

My story-response is a transference interpretation *per metaphor* that offers the possibility that Mattie's efforts to find meaning in his relationship with me need not culminate in empathic failure. It also suggests that my motives and agenda as a therapist may differ substantially from those of Mattie's mother and from other adults with whom he has had such disappointing experiences. Adopting the Charlie persona, I am neither intimidated nor put off by Dominic's lies and bully-like behavior: I am interested, first, in establishing a meaningful interpersonal connection with Dominic and, then, in arriving at a more multidimensional perspective on his real character ("Charlie could see that Dominic wasn't such a terrible guy underneath . . . "); furthermore, I am able to accomplish this without the assistance of a powerful intercessor (Charlie's mother), whose absence from my story conveys my confidence in my professional skills and understanding of the dynamics of his problems.

The intentional repetitiveness of the responding story seems to have enabled Mattie spontaneously to recognize himself in the Dominic character (per his sign-off)—a self-recognition that is rare in the context of metaphorical communications, even among children with greater capacity for self-observation and insight.

Mattie was able to involve himself in our work together with enthusiasm and commitment. Although his therapy ended prematurely when I moved away, he made some very real gains: His antisocial behavior decreased, his sibling conflicts were somewhat reduced, and he demonstrated a greater ability to regulate impulses and to modulate and contain affect. He could not help but experience my departure as yet another loss, but we did have several months in which to explore and work through his attendant disappointment and anger. Ms. R. was undergoing intensive psychotherapy at the same time, and her subsequent improvements had salutary effects on Mattie's emotional well-being.

## COUNTERTRANSFERENCE PHENOMENA

As far as countertransference issues are concerned, there is nothing about the process of reciprocal storytelling to set it apart from any other treatment activity or technique used in the psychotherapy of children. Defined as occurring within an *intersubjective* field, countertransference reactions, fantasies, attitudes, or disjunctive responses are most usefully viewed as arising from the continuous and reciprocal influence between child and clinician.[7] In effect, the child is no more likely to shape the therapist's countertransference reactions than the therapist is to shape the nature of the child's transference experience. On the other hand, the therapist may

---

[7]For a detailed discussion and clinical illustration of the concept of inter-subjectivity in child and adolescent psychotherapy, see J. Brandell (1999).

inadvertently initiate such transference-countertransference sequential chains owing to unresolved conflicts, a perspective that is probably somewhat closer to that of classical psychoanalysis.

Countertransference motives may be at the root of the therapist's failure to understand a child's stories, or of manifestations that involve boredom, confusion, anger, and other strong affects. The potential also exists for the therapist to violate the spirit of the reciprocal interchange by making direct interpretations when there is no strong justification for such a parameter, or by offering responding versions of a child's stories that "work" the material too aggressively. In the latter instance, the child would experience the therapist's story as excessively critical, and feel diminished by it. It can thus be helpful for the therapist to construe responding stories not as correctives but, rather, as wellsprings of new strategies and adaptations for a child, which that child may or may not elect to draw on to expand her or his repertoire of adaptive solutions. Occasionally, a child's lack of interest in or resistance to the reciprocal storytelling procedure, particularly if the same child has participated eagerly in earlier exchanges, is reducible to countertransference features.

## Summary

This chapter explores the phenomenon of transference in the context of reciprocal storytelling. Contemporary psychoanalytic perspectives on the role of interpretation in child psychotherapy and child analysis are reviewed and compared with the potential value of *interpretation within the metaphor* for children with moderately severe, long-standing, and complex psychosocial problems. In particular, the concept of transference in psychoanalytic child therapy, a topic of heated debate for the better part of the last century, is examined, along with various kinds of transferences and transference-like phenomena encountered in clinical work with children.

Moving on to reciprocal storytelling itself, the chapter highlights those qualities that may make children's stories such a potentially valuable medium for the communication of important transference themes, wishes, and fantasies—and, concomitantly, such an effective vehicle for the therapist's transference interpretations.

Indeed, because the therapist's interpretive response is both anticipated and generally well tolerated in reciprocal storytelling, transference interpretations made within the child's metaphor may serve ably as touchstones for more direct and traditional approaches to the interpretation of transference.

# CHAPTER 7

# Is Storytelling Effective? Using Children's Metaphorical Communications to Assess Therapeutic Progress

Reciprocal storytelling has been described here as a highly specialized, psychoanalytically oriented procedure in child psychotherapy used to elicit autogenic stories from children in order to learn more of their disturbing fantasies, conflicts, and defensive adaptations. The child is asked to produce an autogenic or self-composed story that has a beginning, a middle, an end, and perhaps a moral. The therapist then tells a responding story that reworks the thematic material from the child's story and substitutes relatively conflict-free alternative resolutions for the child's maladaptive solutions. Intended for use in

conjunction with other techniques of psychoanalytically oriented child psychotherapy, it has been successfully applied in the treatment of a wide range of
emotional and behavioral disorders, including depression, anxiety disorders, phobias, obsessive-compulsive
problems, difficulties in the regulation of self-esteem,
conduct disorders, and even Gilles des la Tourette's
disorder. More recently, it has been used advanta-
geously to treat children and preadolescents with borderline, schizoid, and selfobject disorders, alexithymia,
and posttraumatic reactions, including those involving
catastrophic loss.

Much of the research literature in the field of dynamic child psychotherapy has focused on the evaluation of treatment effectiveness or outcome where
treatment is globally defined. There has been considerably less interest in *process* research in child psychotherapy, where techniques can be spelled out in
clear and concise terms. However, there may be
some real value in a molecular examination of the di-
verse body of techniques currently classed together
under the umbrella of *psychoanalytically oriented child
psychotherapy*, of which reciprocal storytelling is but
one.

J. L. Despert and H. W. Potter (1936) first advocated adoption of the story told in treatment as a systematic way of assessing therapeutic progress, but
there have been few attempts to do so since. Richard
Gardner (1977, 1993) suggested that therapists utiliz-
ing his *mutual storytelling technique* might make an
impressionistic determination of a child's progress in

treatment by carefully noting whether the child seems to be employing adaptive solutions to conflicts with greater frequency as therapy proceeds. E. Pitcher and E. Prelinger (1963) proposed that the autogenic or stimulus-independent story could be readily used to assess the level of defensive operations, the extent of object relatedness, and prevalent dynamic themes and defenses, but not to evaluate treatment per se.

Impressionistic data and clinical wisdom confirm that as children become able to expand their repertoire of adaptive solutions to conflict, their projective stories will provide the clinician with confirmation of such therapeutic progress. That hypothesis cannot be substantiated without empirical support, however. Accordingly, a quantitative approach for determining how revealing children's stories are as a measure of therapeutic progress or efficacy, and for examining what else they may convey about the nature of the therapeutic process, is described after the following vignette.

## The Case of John

John was an attractive and bright ten-year-old diagnosed, according to established criteria (American Psychiatric Association, 1992), as having an oppositional disorder. He presented with the following symptoms at intake: poor academic performance, temper tantrums, violations of minor rules, provocative behavior, noncompliance, intensive conflict with siblings, pathological lying, and stubbornness.

John's school performance had steadily deteriorated over the past year despite his high intelligence and the combined efforts of both parents and teachers. His parents, who demonstrated a stable marital relationship and expressed concern and frustration over John's declining academic performance and behavior problems, described him as being quite provocative and hostile toward them and his three siblings. John also frequently violated minor rules at home and resorted to temper tantrums when he was unable to get his way. John's father, who emigrated to the United States from western Europe as a young adult, was a successful businessman who spent a great deal of time with all of his children. John's mother functioned principally as a homemaker but participated consistently in both community and church activities. During the initial diagnostic interview with both parents, they freely discussed their own feelings of inadequacy at being unable to help John resolve his problems without treatment. They agreed, however, that professional help was warranted and were quite eager for treatment to begin. John was seen on a twice-weekly basis over a period of several months. A wide assortment of play techniques, including reciprocal storytelling, was used during each therapy session; audiotapes were made of both the child's and therapist's stories as well as of the post-story dialogue.

## DESIGN

Several research instruments were selected for use in this intensive single case study:

- John's diagnosis and his presenting problems suggested considerable difficulty in the control and

adaptive expression of anger. Accordingly, outwardly directed hostility was selected as a major
client process variable, as measured in John's stories
by the *Gottschalk-Gleser Hostility Directed Outward
Scale* (Gottschalk and Gleser, 1969). Treatment
progress with a patient such as John is typically defined both by a reduction in hostility or aggression
*and* by the concomitant substitution of healthier, relatively conflict-free solutions in favor of less adaptive ones. Accordingly, one might expect to see a
measurable decline in the expression of themes involving anger or hostility over the course of therapy.
Two trained raters working independently of each
other analyzed audiotaped transcriptions of John's
stories. The raters were given no information about
him aside from his age and sex, and were similarly
unaware of the actual chronological order of the stories.

• The *Therapist Influence Scale* is an original research instrument (Brandell, 1981) developed specifically to determine the influence of the therapist on the child's
selection of adaptive story elements. Operationally,
this meant that the two raters were provided with transcribed copies of both the child's and the therapist's
stories—although, this time, in their actual chronological order. They were then asked to decide which of the
child's stories displayed evidence of adaptive elements
that appeared in homologous but not identical form in
earlier responding stories of the therapist. For example, the therapist suggested in a responding story told

early in treatment that "angry thoughts can't harm." Several sessions later, John demonstrated that he understood this therapeutic message by resolving a story situation, similar to that in his earlier story, by concluding that "just wishing somebody dead can't really make it happen." In other words, John's moral was quite similar but not identical to the earlier version presented by the therapist. If the moral or lesson was either deemed inappropriate to the content of John's story or appeared to be an exact replication of the earlier moral or lesson of the therapist's, the story was not considered to have been genuinely adaptive.

- The *Parent's Behavior Checklist* (Embry, Leavitt, and Budd, 1975) was administered to John's parents prior to the beginning and at posttermination of their son's treatment (as a pretest and posttest measure). It consisted of forty-five items designed to assess the frequency and severity of problem behaviors.

- The *Children's Psychiatric Rating Scale* (DHEW, 1973) was used to assess the degree of clinically measurable psychopathology both before and after treatment. A separate examiner not otherwise involved in John's therapy administered this instrument.

## Findings

For the purpose of analysis, John's treatment was broken down into three phases representing the beginning, middle, and end of treatment. Outwardly directed hostility for each session was then averaged according to the phase of treatment. Although the story scores varied substantially within all three treatment phases, there appeared to be a downward trend in the expression of outwardly directed hostility across the three treatment phases (see Figure 7.1). This change was also noted on a more impressionistic level by John's psychotherapist.

The raters also agreed that there was increasing evidence of the therapist's corrective influence on the child in John's selection of story adaptations and morals during the middle and end phases of treatment (interscorer reliability = .83).

Visual inspection of the pretest and posttest data for the Children's Psychiatric Rating Scale and the Parent's Behavior Checklist revealed change in a wide range of symptom and behavior areas (see Figures 7.2 and 7.3). These findings tended to serve as confirmatory evidence that the quantitative and impressionistic changes observed in John's stories accurately reflected his overall adjustment. In addition, John's parents reported a significant attenuation of virtually all his original problems at the conclusion of their son's treatment. Informal follow-up several months later revealed that John was continuing to make a good adjustment both at school and at home. Some oppositional trends in John's personality did persist in a milder form, but his parents felt that these trends were primarily adaptive and age-appropriate.

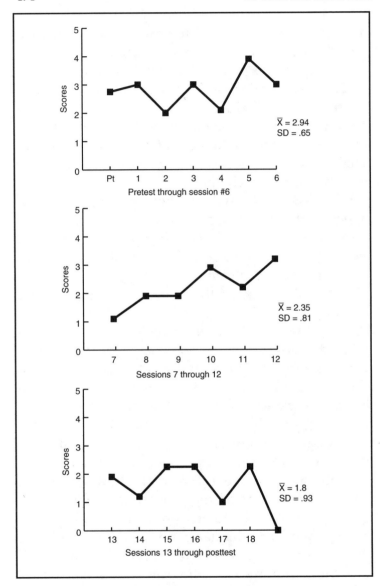

**FIGURE 7.1    Hostility Directed Outward Scores**
SOURCE: Adapted from Gottschalk and Gleser (1969).

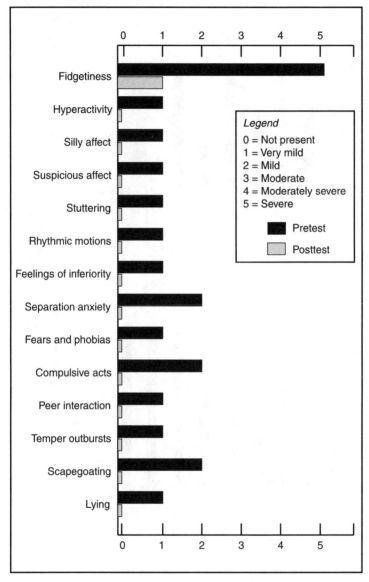

FIGURE 7.2    Children's Psychiatric Rating Scale Items
SOURCE: Adapted from DHEW (1973).

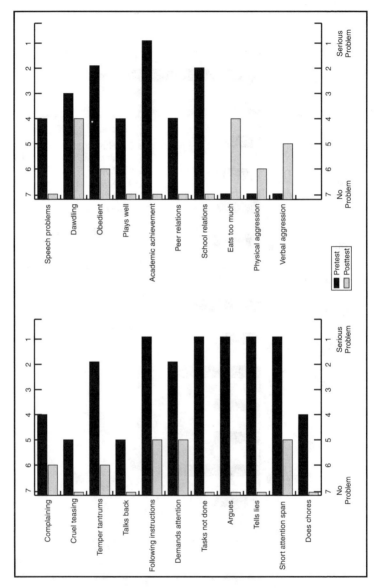

FIGURE 7.3    Parent's Behavior Checklist Items
SOURCE: Adapted from Embry, Leavitt, and Budd (1975).

## THE STORIES

John told twenty stories over the course of treatment (including diagnostic and posttermination stories). Some of his stories reflected preoccupation with separation-individuation issues; others portrayed oedipal ambitions and conflicts, and sibling rivalries; still others gave expression to John's resistance to treatment or to his transference fantasies about the therapist. Overall, the stories exhibited a wide range of content and several different focal conflicts (French & Fromm, 1964; Kepecs, 1977; Brandell, 1987). Despite these differences, however, each of the stories also revealed thematic concern with the expression of anger.

The story that follows, told early in treatment, in many ways typifies John's difficulty in finding relatively conflict-free mechanisms for expressing his anger:

---

### JOHN'S STORY

Once there's this boy who hasn't been doing his schoolwork. And he had homework, lots of it, each day. He never did it and forgot his books at home, because he kept on forgetting everything. When the teacher found out, she gave him five dictionary pages in the back of his spelling book. And he was just staring at the clock instead of working, 'cause it was 5 minutes 'til they could go home. But he didn't know he was going to have to stay after class. When he found out, he got real angry. And so when the teacher had left to get something, he ditched. And he ran off, ran away, got on a bus, got out of town, and he started walking around the streets. And then afterwards [pause] after his teacher had died . . . from can-

cer . . . he was so happy [pause]. He was ten miles
away from this place he had gone to school. He was in
a different city and he decided to go back then, when
he was ninety years old. So, when he was ninety, he
went back on the bus for ten miles. I don't know how
he got the money, but he got all this money out of the
bank, and bought himself a car. And he took lessons,
and he got to drive a car by himself, a Ferrari. That's
the end.

*Moral: Always do your schoolwork and you'll never end up in
trouble.*

## ANALYSIS

The boy in John's story appears to be a relatively
transparent personal representative. The main character in the story, in what appears to be a gesture of
defiance, has not been doing his schoolwork. He not
only fails to do his homework but also continually
forgets to bring his textbooks to school. The character's use of "forgetting" (i.e., repression) can also be
understood as a covert expression of hostility toward the teacher. When the boy in the story learns
that he will have to remain after class, he becomes
enraged with his teacher and flees. The teacher's
death from cancer is another relatively undisguised
expression of the character's rage. It is only after her
death, which occurs when the protagonist is ninety
years old, that it is *finally* safe to return home. The
story suggests that it is dangerous to express angry
feelings, and that they should be contained at all
costs. It also eloquently speaks to how psychologi-

cally crippling such maladaptive solutions to the problem of expressing anger have been for the protagonist. The main character must wait until he is ninety years old in order to learn to drive by himself.

The moral has a cautionary tone as well as a somewhat superficial message. It neither offers insight as to the nature of the boy's conflict nor proposes any new way of coping with the character's hostility. This story, which is drawn from the beginning phase of John's treatment, received a Hostility Directed Outward rating of 2.96, reflecting a moderately high degree of hostile content (see Figure 7.1). The raters further agreed that the story exhibited no measurable therapist influence and utilized solutions to conflict that were both primitive and unrealistic.

John told the next story shortly after the midway point in his treatment. It portrays his continuing struggle over the expression of anger, but with several new elements that clearly differentiate it from stories told earlier in treatment:

_____

JOHN'S STORY

Once there was this boy named Scott. He had lived in Europe, and had his own bicycle, and he was super-good at racing. His bike was a fancy racing bike, a ten-speed. And there was this other boy, whose name was Dick, and he had a five-speed. He wished there was a pile of sand there, and that Scott would skid right over it so he would wipe out. And his bike was just bought, brand new, so if he skidded over, say, a pile of rocks, he could still keep control of his bicycle, because it has new brakes and everything. Anyway, Scott went somewhere without his bike, to America, some place like California, and Dick went out for a ride on his five-speed. He knew Scott was gone, and he went over to Scott's place to see if the garage door was open. Well, it wasn't. It had a lock right there. So, he went home and got a wire, and picked the lock. And Dick started to open the garage door, but then he just shut it because he felt guilty. I mean, if he would have done something wrong to the bike. He was, like, planning on ghost-riding it over a pile of rocks. He was going to make it wipe out, and get it scratched up and stuff. So, he shut the garage door, and he went home and told his mom the whole story.

*Moral: The moral to this story is that wishing is better than really making it happen, and that when you try to do something bad to someone else's thing, somebody else's bike or car, something, you feel guilty. If you're going to rip off a car by hot-wiring it, you [should] shut the door [pause]. You open the door and then you shut it before you can do something [bad] with it.*

## ANALYSIS

This is a story that is not only rich with meaning but also adumbrates John's later and more adaptive efforts at resolving intrapsychic conflict. Both characters in this story seem to serve as self-representatives. Scott is depicted as a kind of idealized self, a loved and talented youngster who owns an expensive bicycle with ten speeds. Dick is portrayed as a competitive, narcissistically vulnerable boy who is envious of Scott's bicycle and, presumably, also of Scott's talents. It may be possible to understand the story as a displacement of the one character's (Dick's) oedipal ambitions and phallic-competitive yearnings toward the other character (Scott), noting in particular the fact that Scott, like John's father, is a European who travels to America. The "ten-speed bicycle," according to such an interpretation, might then symbolize the phallic dominance of the father. In this instance, the core conflict expressed would be one of guilt over the subject's wish to castrate the father (i.e., ruin the fancy bicycle).

The key struggle in this story, however, concerns the narcissistic rage that the main character experiences when his desires are thwarted. The fancy ten-speed bicycle may symbolize a paternal phallus, but at the same time (along with its owner) it is the symbol of an idealized self—one capable of near perfection in all things. Dick feels guilt when his rage and primitive envy, generated by what can only be termed narcissistic mortification, are displaced onto the interpersonal field.

The raters felt that this story reflected John's efforts to deal with his anger more adaptively than in earlier stories—a conclusion that is arguably more important than which of the two interpretations is the more accurate one, even though John's story adaptations at this point in treatment do not yet reveal much insight. However, it is not difficult to recognize a rather primitive attempt at impulse control (i.e., "shutting" the garage door), and a willingness to discuss the conflict openly (i.e., he "told his mom the whole story").

This story was given a lower Hostility Directed Outward rating—1.79—principally because the hostility expressed was of a less overt nature (i.e., characters do not die, nor do they injure, kill, or directly attack each other). It was also judged to have reflected the therapist's corrective influence in the use of story adaptations.

The final story example is drawn from the termination phase of John's treatment. Although John continues to struggle with the problem of anger, the story is in striking contrast to earlier ones told in treatment.

---

## John's Story

There is this one policeman, whose name was Mike, and he was a very nice policeman. He was the head of the crime prevention unit. See, there had been a gang that was disturbing the town and busting down doors and breaking windows and flattening tires, making holdups and stuff. One day there's this man that had been in the gang, and he walked up to Mike. Mike said, "Hello, how are you doing?" And this other man, whose name was Tim, had been a friend of Mike's. He was an undercover agent policeman, but he wasn't supposed to do anything. So he told Mike about something that was really important to him: See, one day the gang had gotten together, like a mob or something, and this guy in the mob said, "Hey, guys, why don't we rob a bank and get rich overnight?" And ten other guys (there was something like twenty guys in the group), these ten guys said, "Yeah, man, let's plan it at our next meeting." And at the next meeting, a couple of days later, Tim—he hadn't ever spoken a word before—said he didn't like the idea of robbing a bank and getting rich overnight. So, he and a few other bad guys set up a different plan. They

decided to try and talk it out or something like that.
They were going to talk about not robbing the bank.
The day that the other bad guys were going to rob the
bank, they had a meeting to plan things. But this big argument started, and all the guys were yelling at each
other and stuff. Finally, Tim managed to say, "Hey,
guys, you know I don't really like the idea of 'getting
rich overnight.'" And a lot of the guys said, "Hey, man,
what do you want to do? What are you, a chicken? Do
you think we're just going to sit around and play hop-
scotch or something like that?" And Tim said, "No, it's
just that I don't like the idea of robbing a bank, because
it's illegal, and we'll get put in jail for the rest of our
lives." So, it turned out that there were other guys who
didn't like the idea of robbing the bank, and there were
more against the plan than for it. Not only that, but the
guys who were against the plan wanted to do something nice, like giving presents or candy to little kids,
and they made up a plan to do that instead.
*Moral: The moral is that it's better not to do something that's
illegal, and if the guys don't listen to you, turn away from
them.*

## ANALYSIS

None of John's stories provides a better or more vivid
example of how the child's identification with the
therapist serves as a vehicle for therapeutic change.
Mike, who heads the crime prevention unit, is an
undisguised therapist-representative in this story. Al-

though Mike is a policeman, he serves as a friendly source of advice for Tim when the latter is in conflict over whether or not to participate in the bank robbery scheme. It is significant that Mike gives no specific advice, however, but is simply available in the beginning of the story as an attuned listener. As this final treatment phase nears its end point, John has gradually begun to acquire more and more of the therapist's functions, thereby enriching his own ego in the process. Although he acknowledges the presence of the therapist in the story, he has already begun the work of depersonifying the therapist's attributes and functions in order to incorporate them as intrapsychic contents.

In his story, John first portrays the strength of his earlier hostile feelings in his (i.e., Tim's) description of the "gang that was disturbing the town and busting down doors and breaking windows." The "gang" seems to stand for John's own projected rage, about which he has gradually developed more awareness in treatment. The story is a particularly good one because John is still moderately ambivalent about what he should be doing with these hostile wishes. Should he go along with the planned robbery and not speak up? Is open defiance of authority an adaptive solution to the problem of expressing anger? Ultimately, Tim decides against the antisocial and hostile act proposed by other members of the gang, and speaks out against the bank robbery scheme. There is also an emphasis on the value of talking out feelings—of giving expression to ideas and emotions even when they arouse conflict. The transparent use of reaction-formation (i.e., doing something nice) observed at the end of the story cannot be called genuinely adaptive. It does, however, demonstrate increased concern over the socially unacceptable nature of unmodified hostility and gives evidence of significant ego activity, whereas little could be observed formerly.

The raters gave this third story a Hostility Directed Outward rating of 1.54, reflecting some thematic concern with aggression, but at a level significantly diminished from that of John's earlier stories. The raters also agreed that there was strong evidence of the therapist's influence present in this termination-phase story.

## SUMMARY

Reciprocal storytelling may be useful not only as a specialized therapeutic technique in dynamic child psychotherapy but also as an instrument for monitoring progress in treatment. Children's autogenic stories are a rich source of information about disturbing wishes and fantasies, characteristic conflicts, and defensive adaptations. Although there is a general consensus that children's projective stories can be understood as metaphorical communications reflecting intrapsychic changes and defensive accommodations in the child over time, little effort has been made to investigate this assumption more thoroughly. Accordingly, one child's stories are featured here. When studied systematically, they prove to be fairly reliable indicators of the magnitude of the child's hostile-aggressive feelings as well as of the extent to which he was able to assimilate the therapist's responses into his own efforts at conflict resolution. Two pretest and posttest measures provide additional evidence in support of John's progress over the course of his treatment, and an anecdotal report made by his mother several months after termination was consistent with both the clinical assessment and the data from the stories. In essence, impressionistic data supplied by John's stories could be confirmed by quantitative means.

# Epilogue

There is, of course, no real magic in stories, even though the storytelling process in and outside of therapy often appears to us to possess magical qualities. Not unlike other techniques and instrumentalities used in psychoanalytic child psychotherapy, reciprocal storytelling taps into a dimension of the child's psychological life not yet overtaken or subverted by the mandates of adult secondary process thinking and logic. However, precisely because children's stories characteristically retain a timeless, metaphoric, and primary process–like quality and yet must possess a certain modicum of structure and consensually based meaning, they are especially well suited for the therapeutic playroom.

In this book, we have examined the value that children's stories appear to hold as a window to the unconscious, a rather unique vantage point from which we are able to view a child's inner world and better understand his or her most perplexing problems and most fervent desires. The child's story, in this sense, is like a secret entrance to the clubhouse from which adults are usually denied access. We soon learn that grown-ups aren't the only ones with ground rules; indeed, the child's invitation to play in the clubhouse can be rescinded at any time. If we are able to remain sensitized to the special requirements of communications made *per metaphor*, the unfolding dialogue can deepen our dynamic understanding and grant us a unique opportunity to assist in the reworking of narrative material in ways that are not only therapeutic but perhaps even transformative.

# References

Abrams, S. (1993). The developmental dimensions of play during treatment: A conceptual overview. In A. Solnit, D. Cohen, and P. Neubauer (Eds.), *The Many Meanings of Play* (pp. 221–228). New Haven: Yale University Press.

Altman, N. (1992). *Relational Perspectives in Psychoanalysis*. Hillsdale, N.J.: Analytic Press.

American Psychiatric Association. (1992). *Diagnostic and Statistical Manual of Mental Disorders*, 4th ed. Washington, D.C.: American Psychiatric Press.

Arlow, J. A., and Kadis, A. (1946). Finger painting in the psychology of children. *American Journal of Orthopsychiatry, 16*, 134–146.

Aurela, A. (1987). A systematic storytelling therapy. *Psychiatrica Fennica, 18*, 31–34.

Bellak, L. (1954). *The TAT and CAT in Clinical Use*. New York: Grune and Stratton.

Bellak, L., and Bellak, S. (1949). *Children's Apperception Test*. Berkeley: C.P.S. Co.

Bender, L., and Woltmann, A. G. (1936). The use of puppet shows as a psychotherapeutic method for behavior problems in children. *American Journal of Orthopsychiatry, 6*, 341–354.

Blos, P., Jr., and Finch, S. (1975). Psychotherapy with children and adolescents. In D. X. Freedman and J. Dyrud (Eds.), *American Handbook of Psychiatry* (pp. 133–162). New York: Basic Books.

Blum, G. (1950). *The Blacky Pictures: A Technique for the Exploration of Personality Dynamics*. New York: The Psychological Corporation.

Brandell, J. (1981). Therapist Influence Scale. Unpublished paper.

_____. (1987). Focal conflict theory: A model for teaching dynamic practice. *Social Casework, 68*, 299–310.

_____. (1988). Storytelling in child psychotherapy. In C. Schaefer (Ed.), *Innovative Interventions in Child and Adolescent Therapy* (pp. 9–44). New York: John Wiley and Sons.

_____. (1999). Countertransference as communication: Intersubjectivity in the treatment of a traumatized adolescent. *Smith College Studies in Social Work, 69*(2), 405–427.

Brandell, J., and Perlman, F. (1997). Psychoanalytic theory. In J. Brandell (Ed.), *Theory and Practice in Clinical Social Work* (pp. 38–80). New York: Free Press/Simon and Schuster.

Brooks, R. (1981). Creative characters: A technique in child therapy. *Psychotherapy: Theory, Research, and Practice, 18*, 131–139.

_____. (1993). Creative characters. In C. Schaefer and D. Cangelosi, *Play Therapy Techniques* (pp. 211–224). Northvale, N.J.: Jason Aronson.

Chethik, M. (2000). *Techniques of Child Therapy*, rev. ed. New York: Guilford Press.

Chused, J. (1988). The transference neurosis in child analysis. *Psychoanalytic Study of the Child, 43*, 51–81.

_____. (1992). The transference neurosis in child analysis. In *Saying Good-bye: A Casebook of Termination in Child and Adolescent Analysis and Therapy,* 233–264. Hillsdale, N.J.: Analytic Press.

Claman, L. (1980). The squiggle drawing-game in child psychotherapy. *American Journal of Psychotherapy, 34*, 414–425.

Cohen, P. M., and Solnit, A. J. (1993). Play and therapeutic action. *Psychoanalytic Study of the Child, 48*, 49–63.

Conn, J. (1939). The child reveals himself through play. *Mental Hygiene, 23*, 49–69.

_____. (1941). The treatment of fearful children. *American Journal of Orthopsychiatry, 11*, 744–751.

_____. (1948). The play interview as an investigative and therapeutic procedure. *The Nervous Child, 7*, 257–286.

Davis, J. (1986). Storytelling using the child as consultant. *Elementary School Guidance Counselor, 21*, 89–94.

Despert, J. L., and Potter, H. W. (1936). Technical approaches in the study and treatment of emotional problems in childhood. *Psychoanalytic Quarterly, 10*, 619–638.

DHEW (Department of Health, Education, and Welfare). (1973). Pharmacotherapy of children. *Psychopharmacology Bulletin* [Special Issue], p. 196. Rockville, Md.: DHEW (HSM) 73–9002.

Di Leo, J. (1973). *Children's Drawings as Diagnostic Aids.* New York: Brunner/Mazel.

Dreikurs, R. (1975). Basic principles in dealings with children. In R. Dreikurs et al. (Eds.), *Adlerian Family Counseling* (pp. 23–31). Eugene: University of Oregon Press.

Ekstein, R. (1966). *Children of Time and Space, of Action and Impulse.* New York: Appleton-Century-Crofts.

Elkind, D. (1989). *The Hurried Child: Growing Up Too Fast Too Soon.* New York: Addison Wesley Longman.

Elson, M. (1986). *Self Psychology in Clinical Social Work.* New York: Norton and Company.

Embry, L., Leavitt, S., and Budd. R. (1975). Parent Training Check Lists. (Unpublished manuscript.)

Engel, S. (1999). *The Stories Children Tell: Making Sense of the Narratives of Childhood.* New York: W. H. Freeman and Co.

Erikson, E. (1959). *Childhood and Society.* New York: W. W. Norton and Co.

_____. (1977). *Toys and Reasons.* New York: W. W. Norton and Co.

Eth, S., and Pynoos, R. (1985). *Posttraumatic Stress Disorder in Children.* Washington, D.C.: American Psychiatric Association Press.

Finch, S. (1960). *Fundamentals of Child Psychiatry.* New York: Norton.

Fonagy, P., et al. (1996). Il transfert e la sua interpretazione (On transference and its interpretation). *Richard e Piggle,* 4, 255–273.

Fonagy, P., and Target, M. (1998). Mentalization and the changing aims of child psychoanalysis. *Psychoanalytic Dialogues,* 8, 87–114.

Fraiberg, S. (1965). A comparison of the analytic method in two stages of a child analysis. *Journal of the American Academy of Child Psychiatry,* 4, 387–400.

French, T., and Fromm, E. (1964). *Dream Interpretation: A New Approach.*

Freud, A. (1929). *Introduction to the Technique of Child Analysis.* New York/Washington, D.C.: Nervous and Mental Disease Publishing Co.

Freud, A. (1946). *The Psychoanalytic Treatment of Children*. New York: International Universities Press.

Freud, A. (1965). Normality and pathology in childhood. *The Writings of Anna Freud*, Vol. 6 (pp. 25–53). New York: International Universities Press.

Freud, S. (1900 [1973]). The interpretation of dreams. *Standard Edition*, 4, 127–133.

Freud, S. (1923 [1973]). The ego and the id. *Standard Edition, 19,* 12–26.

Freud, S., and Breuer, J. (1895 [1973]). Studies on hysteria. *Standard Edition, 2.*

Fromm-Reichmann, F. (1950). *Principles of Intensive Psychotherapy*. Chicago: University of Chicago Press.

Gabel, S. (1984). The draw a story game: An aid in understanding and working with children. *The Arts in Psychotherapy, 11,* 187–196.

Gardner, R. (1977). *Therapeutic Communication with Children: The Mutual Storytelling Technique, 2nd ed.* New York: Jason Aronson.

_____. (1993). *Storytelling in Psychotherapy with Children*. Northvale, N.J.: Jason Aronson.

Giovacchini, P. (1992). The severely disturbed adolescent. In J. Brandell (Ed.), *Countertransference in Psychotherapy with Children and Adolescents* (pp. 141–162). Northvale, N.J.: Jason Aronson.

Gondor, L. (1957). Use of fantasy communications in child psychotherapy. *American Journal of Psychotherapy, 5,* 323–335.

Gottschalk, L. A., and Gleser, G. C. (1969). The measurement of psychological states through the content analysis of human behavior. *Manual of Instructions for Using the Gottschalk-Gleser Content Analysis Scales: Anxiety, Hostility and Social Alienation-Personal Disorganization*. Berkeley: University of California Press.

Greenspan, S. (1983). *The Clinical Interview of the Child*. New York: McGraw-Hill.

Hawkey, L. (1951). The use of puppets in child psychotherapy. *British Journal of Medical Psychology, 24,* 206–214.

Hug-Hellmuth, H. von. (1913). *Aus dem Seelenleben des Kindes*. Leipzig: Deuticke.

_____. (1921). On the technique of child analysis. *International Journal of Psycho-Analysis, 2,* 287–305.

Kepecs, J. (1977). Teaching psychotherapy by use of brief transcripts. *American Journal of Psychotherapy, 31*, 383–393.

Kestenbaum, C. (1985). The creative process in child psychotherapy. *American Journal of Psychotherapy, 39*, 479–489.

Klein, M. (1932). *The Psychoanalysis of Children.* London: Hogarth Press.

Kohut, H. (1977). *The Restoration of the Self.* New York: International Universities Press.

_____. (1984). *How Does Analysis Cure?* Edited by A. Goldberg and P. Stepansky. Chicago: University of Chicago Press.

Kritzberg, N. (1971). TASKIT (Tell-a-story-kit), the therapeutic story-telling word-game. *Acta Paedopsychiatrica, 38*, 231–234.

_____. (1975). *The Structured Therapeutic Game Method of Child Analytic Psychotherapy.* Hicksville, N.Y.: Exposition Press.

Krystal, H. (1993). *Integration and Self-Healing: Affect, Trauma, Alexithymia.* Hillsdale, N.J.: The Analytic Press.

Lawson, D. (1987). Using therapeutic stories in the counseling process. *Elementary School Guidance Counselor, 12*, 134–141.

Lieberman, F. (1983). Work with children. In D. Waldfogel and A. Rosenblatt (Eds.), *Handbook of Clinical Social Work* (pp. 441–465). San Francisco: Jossey-Bass.

Liebowitz, J. (1972). Storytelling in search of a plot. *Reiss-Davis Clinical Bulletin, 9*, 112–115.

Lourie, R., and Rieger, R. (1972). Psychiatric and psychological examination of children. In S. Arieti et al. (Eds.), *The American Handbook of Psychiatry.* New York: Basic Books.

Mahler, M., Pine, F., and Bergman, A. (1975). *The Psychological Birth of the Human Infant.* New York: Basic Books.

Marcus, I. (1966). Costume play therapy: The exploration of a method for stimulating imaginative play in older children. *Journal of Child Psychiatry, 5*, 441–452.

Masterson, J. ( 1972). *Treatment of the Borderline Adolescent: A Developmental Approach.* New York: Wiley.

McDougall, J. (1984). The dis-affected patient: Reflections on affect pathology. *Psychoanalytic Quarterly, 53*, 386–409.

_____. (1985). *Theaters of the Mind.* New York: Basic Books.

_____. (1989). *Theaters of the Body.* New York: Basic Books.

Millar, S. (1974). *The Psychology of Play.* New York: Jason Aronson.

Mishne, J. (1992). Treatment of borderline children and adolescents. In J. Brandell (Ed.), *Countertransference in Psychotherapy with Children and Adolescents* (pp. 235–265). Northvale, N.J.: Jason Aronson.

Mitchell, S., and Black, M. (1995). *Freud and Beyond: A History of Modern Psychoanalytic Thought.* New York: Basic Books.

Neubauer, P. (1993). Playing: Technical implications. In A. J. Solnit, D. J. Cohen, and P. B. Neubauer (Eds.), *The Many Meanings of Play* (pp. 44–53). New Haven: Yale University Press.

_____. (1994). The role of displacement in psychoanalysis. *Psychoanalytic Study of the Child, 49,* 107–119.

Piaget, J. (1969). *The Psychology of the Child.* New York: Basic Books.

Pitcher, E., and Prelinger, E. (1963). *Children Tell Stories: An Analysis of Fantasy.* New York: International Universities Press.

Rambert, M. (1949). *Children in Conflict.* New York: International Universities Press.

Rhue, J., and Lynn, S. (1991). *The International Journal of Clinical and Experimental Hypnosis, 39,* 198–214.

Rinsley, D. (1980). Diagnosis and treatment of borderline and narcissistic children and adolescents. *Bulletin of the Menninger Clinic, 44,* 147–170.

Roberts, G. (1982). *Roberts Apperception Test for Children.* Los Angeles: Western Psychological Services.

Robertson, M., and Barford, F. (1970). Story-making in psychotherapy with a chronically ill child. *Psychotherapy: Theory, Research, and Practice, 7,* 104–107.

Robson, K. (1983). *The Borderline Child: Approaches to Etiology, Diagnosis, and Treatment.* New York: McGraw-Hill.

Sandler, J., Kennedy, H., and Tyson, R. (1980). *The Technique of Child Psychoanalysis: Discussions with Anna Freud.* London: Hogarth.

Schafer, R. (1980). Narration in the psychoanalytic dialogue. *Critical Inquiry, 7,* 29–53.

_____. (1997). *Tradition and Change in Psychoanalysis.* Madison, Conn.: International Universities Press.

Simmons, J. (1969). *Psychiatric Examination of Children.* Philadelphia: Lea and Febiger.

Socor, B. (1993). The self after thought: An object relations discussion of a failure to know. *Journal of Analytic Social Work, 1,* 75–104.

Solomon, J. (1938). Active play therapy. *American Journal of Orthopsychiatry, 8,* 479–498.

_____. (1940). Active play therapy: Further experiences. *American Journal of Orthopsychiatry, 10,* 763–781.

_____. (1951). Therapeutic use of play. In H. Anderson and G. Anderson (Eds.), *An Introduction to Projective Techniques* (pp. 639–661). Englewood Cliffs, N.J.: Prentice-Hall.

Spence, D. (1982). *Narrative Truth and Historical Truth: Meaning and Interpretation in Psychoanalysis.* New York: W. W. Norton and Co.

Starr, A. (1977). *Rehearsal for Living: Psychodrama.* Chicago: Nelson-Hall.

Tolpin, M., and Kohut, H. (1980). The disorders of the self: The psychopathology of the first years of life. In S. Greenspan and G. Pollock, (Eds.), *The Course of Life: Psychoanalytic Contributions Toward Understanding Personality Development* (pp. 425–442). Rockville, Md.: National Institute of Mental Health.

Tyson, P. (1978). Transference and developmental issues in the analysis of a prelatency child. *Psychoanalytic Study of the Child, 33,* 213–236.

Tyson, P., and Tyson, R. (1986). The concept of transference in child psychoanalysis. *Journal of the American Academy of Child Psychiatry, 25,* 30–39.

Viderman, S. (1979). The analytic space: Meaning and problems. *Psychoanalytic Quarterly, 48,* 257–291.

Wilden, A. (1968). *The Language of the Self: The Function of Language in Psychoanalysis.* Baltimore: Johns Hopkins University Press.

Winnicott, D. (1971). *Therapeutic Consultations in Child Psychiatry.* New York: Basic Books.

Woltmann, A. (1940). The use of puppets in understanding children. *Mental Hygiene, 24,* 445-458.

_____. (1950). Mud and clay: Their functions as developmental aids and as media of projection. In N. Wolff (Ed.), *Personality: Symposia on Topical Issues* (pp. 35–50). New York: Grune and Stratton.

_____. (1951). The use of puppetry as a projective method in therapy. In H. Anderson and G. Anderson (Eds.), *An Introduction to Projective Techniques and Other Devices for Understanding the Dynamics of Human Behavior* (pp. 192–209). New York: Prentice-Hall.

Yanof, J. A. (1996). Language, communication, and transference in child analysis. *Journal of the American Psychoanalytic Association, 44,* 79–116.

Zeanah, C., Anders, T., Seifer, R. and Stern, D. (1989). Implications of research in infant development for psychodynamic theory and practice. *Journal of the American Academy of Child and Adolescent Psychiatry, 28,* 657–688.

# Index

---